The Human Art
of Counseling

The Human Art of Counseling

Joseph Simons
& Jeanne Reidy

Herder and Herder

1971
HERDER AND HERDER NEW YORK
232 Madison Avenue, New York 10016

.

Library of Congress Catalog Card Number: 73-165501
© 1971 by Herder and Herder, Inc.
Manufactured in the United States

Contents

To Carl Rogers,
a human counselor

The crucial point is that I confront the patient as one human being to another.

C. G. Jung

Introduction

This book is for anyone, professional or non-professional, who counsels other people and who is concerned about that counseling. This book, then, is for teachers, lawyers, clergymen, nurses, staff members in clinics and hospitals, homemakers, group facilitators, psychologists—for anyone, in or out of these categories, whom others approach as "someone I can talk to."

Often these counselors, when they are approached by a person seeking help, feel bungling and inadequate. They decry their ignorance of technique, their lack of knowledge, their insufficient understanding of psychology. "I'm not a psychologist." "I don't know what to say." "I don't want to hurt anyone." "What would a real counselor say?"

Having shared all these feelings about counseling, we authors express in this book what we have found to be helpful in our own counseling experience and in our work with persons preparing to do counseling as part of their lives as teachers, clergymen, homemakers. We center the book on what we consider the basis of counseling success: the counselor's humanity and his own relationship with his client. We have found in our own experience and in the experience of others that counseling seems to go best when the counselor has learned to recognize and trust hrs own feelings and responses, and has taken the large risk of allowing himself to interact honestly with the person who seeks his help. This book suggests the following guideline: "Be yourself in relationship with this person who comes to you for help."

Sometimes a person whom others approach for counsel feels disqualified by his own humanity. He considers himself a failure as a counselor because, when a person comes to him for help, he discovers that he himself begins to feel too much, to get involved, to experience fear and bewilderment. He discovers that he can't classify this person, that he is not prepared to figure out this client's problems or personality. Confused and discouraged, he wants to give up. Or, if he does not give up, he may at any rate allow the most helpful and healing equipment he possesses to go to waste in the very presence of the person seeking help. He ignores his own humanity.

The teacher, faced with a high school student's despair and hatred; the psychologist in the counseling center who panics in the face of a client's love; the nurse who discovers she is losing sleep over the psychic relapses of a patient; the lawyer who finds that his clients are human beings in need of a communication unmentioned by the law books; all these persons, caught short in their attempt to help others, may consider their own human responses their worst enemies. Or they may overlook these responses and wonder why their counseling seems to be heading toward failure.

This book is an attempt to speak to counselors, not about their professional preparation, their diagnoses, or their schools of thought, but about their own humanity as it appears in the counseling situation. We would like to share with these counselors our own experiences in the hope that discovering the emotions in fellow workers may bring some illumination and encouragement. In writing the book and especially in addressing the fellow counselor directly, we realize we may be violating some individual concepts of conventional psychology and traditional psychotherapy. But at the risk of incurring disapproval, we wish to offer what may prove to be assistance in an area where counseling books are often of little help. We therefore address you, the counselor, and we wish to discuss with you your humanity as it comes into play when you sit down to talk with a person seeking your help.

Some Words

In this book we will use words such as "counselor," "client," and "interview." These can be technical terms in psychotherapy, but they can also bear broader meanings. By "counselor" we mean a help-giver—any person to whom another person comes for help in living his life. Many of the counselors spoken of in this book would not use the title for themselves. "I'm not really a counselor. People just seem to want to talk to me about their problems."

By the word "client" we refer to any person who comes to these counselors for help. These so-called "clients" could be students approaching a teacher for advice on more than their studies. They could be patients in a hospital or clinic who find that a nurse or a nurse-aide is "someone I can really talk to." "She understands." "Thanks to her visits, I feel much better about things generally and I think I can work my way out of this depression." These so-called clients could be actual legal clients coming to a lawyer about making a will or about a threatened lawsuit. "I guess maybe I ought to make out a will, but it seems kind of weird. I'm a pretty healthy guy." "If this goes to trial, I'm finished. I'm done for." In the midst of their fears and evasions, they may find that their lawyer really hears them; perhaps for the first time they feel "noticed"; and they begin to speak to the lawyer, not as a master of cases, but as a human being who understands their real plight and who is humanly touched by it. The list of these so-called clients is endless. These persons could be a spouse, an employee, a fellow student, a fellow worker, a neighbor, a friend, and so on. Many of these "clients" would balk at the name. We will use the word simply for convenience.

"Interview" is another word we will use more broadly than in a technical sense. By "interview" we will mean any kind of contact between persons, one of whom is seeking personal help from the other. This contact could be a regular weekly interview, one hour long, occurring by appointment. On the other hand, it could be a chance meeting. It could be a conversation during a lunch hour or during a professional visit or during work hours or after dinner at home. A series of such contacts could be scheduled or unscheduled, planned or unplanned, long or short. These contacts could have or not have a time limit. In other words, the word "interview" in this book has several uses centering on the central meaning of a "helpful human contact between persons."

The Human Art
of Counseling

1. The Counseling Relationship

Counseling has a human beginning. Someone has been attracted to you as a person. He has sensed in you the possibility of understanding and assistance. He has strong hope that you will not repulse him if he approaches you for help. He has discovered your humanity and has already felt related to you. And so, sometimes long before he asks your help, you and the client have begun the relationship whose development is central to counseling.

Then he asks to see you. The student stops you outside class and asks if he could talk to you sometime "not about school—about, well—*could* I talk to you sometime?" Or as you are leaving the hospital room, the patient mentions some personal difficulty and asks if you would let him speak to you about it. Sometimes no appointment is made: the person just starts talking. For example, the man in your law office cannot find the right words and, in embarrassment, finally looks to you for some understanding of his total plight.

At the moment of the request for help, then, you are already in communication with a person who finds in you a promise of understanding and assistance. The human relationship between you is already alive. The spoken or unspoken request for help has also expressed confidence in you. One human being has said to you, "I am now in relationship with you. I feel we have made contact and can continue to make contact. I am hoping you will keep on responding." This is an act of affirmation of the human being you are and of your ability to notice another human being. From the beginning you as a human person, and the human relationship between you and the one seeking your help, are central to the counseling. It was your own self that attracted the person, inspired his confidence, and encouraged him to risk asking your help. The conclusion is: trust your own human self.

What might be your responses when this person asks your help? Perhaps they are a mixture of pleasure, fear, hope, and lack of self-confidence. It may help to tell the person how you feel: you are happy that he asked you; his request makes you feel important; you like him and want to help him; you are afraid you will fail him, but you are willing to try to help. If your inner response is, "No, not another one! I just don't have time," then it seems best to say this right away to the person. Perhaps you can see him at some later date or perhaps you cannot take on this "counseling" at all. Better to tell him honestly from the beginning what your feelings are than to allow a false or forced relationship to develop. Perhaps your response is a combination: "No, not another one!—Yet this one I want to help." Better to express this combination of feelings. Your honesty, while possibly bringing some hurt and disappointment, has brought the person what first attracted him—your human self.

The Human rather than the Professional Relationship

The relationship begins. The student enters your office at the appointed time; or you come to the patient's room; or your friend sits down in the family room for the heart-to-heart talk you had planned. At that moment the emotions, instincts, and histories of both of you come into play. The relationship already existing between you now undergoes changes, and these changes can be changes of growth or changes of deterioration. We are saying that growth in the relationship should result if you sincerely try to be your own plain self, the self that attracted this person's confidence. We are suggesting that you remain aware of your own emotions and responses during this interview, that you express yourself honestly even at considerable risk, and that you attend to the person before you as a person in relationship with you, not as an object to be shaped according to some predetermined rules.

Your primary temptation in this first talk will be to distrust this real self of yours. For you seem to be asked immediately to assume a definite role which can alter your view of yourself and the client and can direct your words away from your real feelings. The tempting role is that of "helper." You can even call it "counselor" or "informal therapist." Whatever the name, the role is real and is a threat to your being yourself with this person.

After all, the person has come for help; you are there to help. The relationship between you seems primarily that of help-seeker to help-giver. And so you assume the role with its attitudes, guidelines, and responses. Your thinking, your self-awareness, your observation of the client are all channeled in a certain direction. You assume the role of someone who wants to find out what this person's problem is and how you can bring help through illumination and guidance.

In responding to your role of helper, you may spend the first hour trying to "figure out" this person, attempting to pick out the symptoms of his disturbance, trying to solve his problem. You do not so much hear him as listen for clues. You are aware of yourself as a problem solver and not as an emotional human person. You are, of course, ceasing to be fully yourself, and you are focusing on a relationship which falls short of the fully human and personal. Assuming this helper role can prove injurious; you cease to some extent to be the person he had reached out to.

In the helper role, you may center immediately on the problem that the person states. This problem might deal with marriage difficulties, career problems, school choices. You may ask questions about the difficulty, seek the person's attitudes, and then attempt to find some helpful solutions. Or, knowing that solutions may not be immediately possible, you may attempt to discover directions which might alleviate the difficulties and lead toward a good outcome. Often too the client is only too ready to let you assume the role of helper while he plays his part of help-seeker, especially when you address yourself to his immediate problem. He really thinks that all he wants is an almost

computerized answer; he often really thinks all he wants
of you is your superior knowledge or experience. Sometimes he will allude to your role of help-giver by saying,
"By now you probably have me all figured out." "Well,
that's the problem. Now what do I do?"

Although it is possible that you will satisfy the client
and bring him the assistance he needs by answering questions, it is also possible that you will, by assuming the
helper role, remove yourself from being what he really
needs and from giving him what he is really, if unconsciously, asking for. When a person comes to you for
counseling, he is usually a person dissatisfied with himself,
uncomfortable and anxious, and in some way at odds with
others who surround him daily. Human relations for him
are often difficult and discouraging.

And now he is coming to you. He has been attracted
to you personally and he has sensed that you and he can
communicate. He has moreover a good reason to talk
to you because he has a recognizable problem which you,
seen as counselor, accept as a fair way to get in contact
with you. It's all right to come to you with a problem.
Put more accurately: it's all right for him, under these
circumstances now, to come to you. He has an acceptable
reason to be with you and to ask your attention. You have
a reason to enter into a relationship with him. Often, and
often unknown to himself, what he really wants is not a
solution to a problem; he wants a friend. His problem is
his entrance fee into your life. If you remain in a helper
role, even while it is the role he thinks he wants you in,
you may never reach your client nor bring him lasting
help. The client is usually somewhere within himself,
asking you to give him yourself. He is asking you to be

that human being who noticed him and seemed able to touch him. He is asking you to be this human self, and precisely as this self, to accept him as he really is. His plea is not small. It demands risk of both of you. To ignore it is the first pitfall of counseling.

Developing the Human Relationship

If, from the beginning, you allow yourself to respond humanly to the person before you, then you are setting a certain pattern for the following conversations and for the whole relationship between you. You give a direction to your own interests. What you see in the client is not an object whose improvement you are working on, but a person, a kind of friend. What primarily commands your attention is not the client's achievements, but this person, his actual here-and-now self. Although his successes and his failures are important to you, they are not your main concern. For, whether he achieves something or not, he himself remains worthwhile.

Such an attitude in you can also set a pattern for the client's responses. If he is, consciously or not, asking you for friendship, he will pick up the signals that tell him you are interested in him, not as a case but as a person. He will sooner or later catch the tone that he is not just another member of the category "student" or "patient" or "advisee"; to you he is himself, this human person, and you are willing to be his friend. His own person attracts you; his own person can be accepted by you and can contact you. Perhaps then he himself can look with more acceptance and trust to the person he is. Perhaps he can find courage to explore that often dark and confusing self. For he is with a friend, and that friend finds value in him.

If, on the other hand, you do not allow yourself to be human during this first conversation, you can set quite another pattern for the relationship between you and the client. You will tend to treat this person as an object to be studied, analyzed, worked on, and cured. Or you will focus on him merely as "someone to be helped." Not wishing to become emotionally involved, you will probably set a tone of aloofness. You will not attend to your own feelings of affection, interest, anger, aversion, worry, and care. You will set up a different kind of relationship where friendship is not a consideration.

Again the client will probably pick up the signals. He is a "case" now, and cases have classifications, symptoms, problems, and outcomes. He may focus immediately on these symptoms or these problems. His hopes may center on solutions. But at the same time, whether consciously or not, he may experience a new failure in human relationships. He has a background of such failures; here is another one. You will not be his friend; he is not worthy; he is not valuable to you as a person but as a case. Once again his inward cry has not been heard. He may sense this without even realizing that he has an inward cry or at least what it is within him that wants to be heard. He may approve what you are doing for him, but something deep remains awry. While you may certainly bring him much help, your personal aloofness may keep you from touching upon his more radical needs.

Risks in the Human Relationship

There are risks you take if you decide to respond humanly to the client during your first contact. First of all, you risk frightening him away. He may not return to you for counseling. For it can be a fearsome thing to be addressed with openness and sincerity on a personal level. After all, roles and façades provide a kind of protection and security. In their absence, one real self addresses another real self, and this manner of address is not customary. If in this relationship you remain aware of your own feelings; if these are feelings of interest, affection, and concern; and if you express your attitude honestly, you are indeed offering yourself to this other person and you are addressing, not his role or his façades, but his real and often hidden inner self. The client, faced with this candor, might panic. It may seem to him much safer to have you perform as "helper" and to remain himself in the role of "case." Person-to-person relationship can bring great threats, even to one who longs for such a relationship. The client may fear self-exploration so much that when faced with a person who addresses him on the level of his real self, he will throw up his defenses and refuse to go further. Although he may long for personal contact and gropes to find it, when he is faced with its risky and embarrassing actuality, he cannot accept it. The outcome, then, of your human approach may be that the client decides not to return for another talk.

Another risk you take if you respond humanly in the first interview is this: you yourself may have to discontinue the counseling. You may find that you cannot relate well to this person. If you allow yourself to feel and to respond honestly, you may discover that you feel an aversion toward this person. You are not drawn to him; you experience difficulty in hearing him fairly. You do not feel that you can be a friend to him. If you tried to enter a personal relationship with this person, you would force feelings you do not have, and you would give insincere responses. If this is the case, then it seems best in the very beginning to suggest to the client that he find someone else to talk to. You may tell him that you certainly want to help him but you feel that you are not the one who can. Although you risk hurting the person, that risk seems worth taking in view of the alternative which could bring greater hurt to both of you. Telling the client how you feel and terminating the counseling will usually be costly to you personally. Having someone seek you out for help is an affirmation of your person. It is hard to refuse the further affirmation this person might bring. But the choice on one level is simple: do you or do you not want to be honest with the people who come to you for help?

Examples

Here are some examples of first interviews in which the counselor made some attempt to be human with the person asking help.

During his first three semesters at college, Jack, a

pre-med student, had received high grades. But right before the final examinations of his fourth semester, he
began to experience intense fears of failure. He felt sure
he would not pass the exams. Distraught, he went to Mr.
Carter, a favorite teacher who had been his chemistry
instructor the year before and with whom he felt at ease
and free to talk.

He told Mr. Carter of his fears. "I know I'm going
to flunk. I just know it. I'm so upset about it I can't concentrate. I open a book and nothing happens. I just panic.
What can I do?"

After some questions, Mr. Carter could see that there
were no solid reasons for Jack's fear of failure. His test
grades had been good during the semester, his lab work
successful, his class attendance regular. Yet despite all
this evidence to the contrary, Jack was obviously terrified
that he would fail. And if the terror continued, there was
a chance that he would not be able to handle the examinations well.

Mr. Carter reflected for a few moments. His first
impulse was to attempt to reassure Jack. He could re-
count all the evidence of probable success, and then tell
the boy not to worry. But then he realized that such reassurance would mean nothing, and would only say to
Jack, "You don't understand." Nor would he touch the
real problem if he said, "Why don't you stop studying for
a while, and go play ball." Or, "Maybe you need a study
schedule or some help from another student who could
quiz you and show you that you do know the course
material." Such advice seemed remote from what was
going on in Jack.

Sensing the irrelevance of such attempts to reassure

or divert, Mr. Carter did not address himself immediately to the boy's study problem. He decided instead to express his own feelings about what Jack was saying. He said, "I know you get good grades, and that scholastically you actually have nothing to worry about. My first impulse is to tell you not to worry, and to go play ball or something. But all that advice seems way off the mark. You are suffering, and suffering quite a bit. I really feel for you. I sense your fear, and I know from my own experience that a fear like that can tear you apart."

At this, Jack interrupted with a "Thanks! I appreciate that. I do feel awful." He seemed to be saying, "You are taking me seriously."

Mr. Carter continued: "Frankly, my feeling is that your problem is not a study problem. I feel your fear of tests may be only what the fear looks like on the outer edge. I'm confused; I'm wondering what is really making you upset. I know I could be all wrong, and I fear I might be. Maybe your whole trouble *is* just about study and concentrating. But I have the feeling that something else is at the root of your fears. If you would like to talk more about this, I'd be glad to listen and try to help. Otherwise, all I have to say is, your fears are irrational, you won't flunk, so go play ball and forget about the tests. But I would be sorry to leave you with such empty advice."

Jack hesitated and then said, "Let's talk some more."

At this Mr. Carter again shared his feelings: "I am wondering why these tests mean so much to you."

"I want to be a doctor. If I don't get good grades, I can't get into med school."

Again Mr. Carter could have reassured Jack that his

grades were good enough to get him into med school. But instead of giving this reassurance, Mr. Carter continued the questioning. "Why is it so important that you get into med school?"

"Lots of reasons. But I guess maybe it's mostly my parents. It means so much to them. They've sacrificed a lot for me so I could get into college and be a doctor. That's their one big wish—to see me a doctor. They've talked about it since I was a kid, and I don't want to let them down."

As the conversation continued, Jack began to examine more closely his relationship with his parents and his attention to their wishes. He found difficulty in admitting that he might have some feelings for them that were, in his own words, "not too pretty." He also mentioned some fears he had about becoming a doctor. "I usually don't talk this way," he explained, "because I intend to become a doctor no matter what." But, he said, he did sometimes in his "weak moments" consider some other kinds of work that would be easier and more attractive for him personally. But being a doctor did remain for him, he said, "the ideal." It seemed a demanding ideal, a kind of ascetic punishment, an "ordeal" in the old sense, which would somehow prove that he was worth something. Another profession that attracted him was, he said, "for queers only, and I'm not a queer."

At the close of this conversation, Jack seemed still worried and upset, but he also had a healthy confusion. He thanked Mr. Carter profusely and arranged for another conversation after the tests. He did return and, in company with Mr. Carter, began to face and deal with a host of previously well-concealed emotions and attitudes. Thanks to Mr. Carter's sensing and expressing his own human responses to the boy's problems in the first interview, the two of them had been able to center their attention then and later on the far more complex difficulties which were hidden beneath an irrational worry over some upcoming exams.

*   *   *

Sometimes being a human counselor in the first contact does not have such happy results. As we mentioned before, if you try to be yourself and to respond to this person honestly and openly, you risk frightening him away. It is no small event for him to see you without the expected façades. You are just there, obviously caring about him, interested, perhaps a little weary or bored, but willing to develop the affection already existing between you. According to social custom, you would be expected to reveal none of this to a stranger. What custom asks is an accepted pattern of professional attentiveness. Nor do the client's façades win you over. You address his real self, the self that shows fear or loneliness or affection or embarrassment or confusion. In fact he probably tries to conceal this self for he is sure no one can care about it. And here you are, speaking to that self, accepting its existence, asking its response to your own disclosed self. The experience is so risky for both of you that the client—and even you—can decide that it is better to drop the relationship.

A lawyer, responding honestly to a new client, may be baffled by the facts and their explanations as the client presents them. At the same time the lawyers may have noticed several signs of embarrassment, fear, protectiveness, pretended good humor lightly covering defiance or sorrow. The client seems to be concealing even from himself the more real but perhaps painful situation. Instead of assuming the customary professional façade, the lawyer expresses his confusion and wonder, and tells the client of his interest, sympathy, and even fear for him. At this the client, incensed, says, "I need a lawyer, not a psychiatrist," and leaves the office, never to return.

A doctor, having examined a patient with constipation difficulties, realizes there is little physical basis for the condition. But during the office visit and the examination he has noticed tensions, fears, and worries in the patient's face, posture, and conversation. While he is discussing the examination results with the patient, he mentions his concern about the tension he has observed. He may suggest that, in his view, these fears could well contribute to the constipation difficulties. Perhaps the patient's response is, "At last somebody understands!" On the other hand, perhaps the response is, "This doctor is trying to tell me I'm neurotic. He isn't seeing how really sick I am. I probably have cancer, and here he is telling me it's all in my head." And the patient seeks a new doctor who "will take my illness seriously."

*   *   *

Gary, a high school senior, liked and trusted Mrs. Alvarez, his English teacher. He liked to drop by her classroom to discuss books or to ask her commentary on

papers he had written for class. Although Gary was a
fluent talker, Mrs. Alvarez suspected that he had few
friends and that he lived a good bit of his day in a
fantasy world. He liked to talk about his little brother
and about his own childhood, but he seldom mentioned
any conversations or good times with young people his
own age. Mrs. Alvarez felt real affection for Gary and
was glad he liked and trusted her.

One afternoon Gary asked if he could stop by to discuss the critical comments Mrs. Alvarez had written on
one of his short stories. When he appeared for the interview, however, he tossed the paper on a chair and said,
"You know, there's a lot more I'd like to talk to you
about. Somehow I can really talk to you. And—well, I'm
confused, and—you know, I don't know what to do.
Something's wrong, and I thought maybe you could
help me."

Mrs. Alvarez said she was pleased that he would ask
her help. "I like you very much, Gary, and I worry about
you. It would mean a lot to me to hear about your confusions."

Gary looked away and began rubbing his fingers on the
desk top. Then suddenly he began talking of some confusions he had about the last novel they had read for class.
Seeming to address the blank wall behind Mrs. Alvarez,
he had switched the conversation away from the personal
onto their usual topic of books. Mrs. Alvarez, disappointed at this turn, interrupted to tell Gary, "I wonder
if those are the confusions you meant when you first
came in. I'd be glad to discuss the novel with you, but I
will be disappointed. I wanted us to talk about you."

Her statements seemed to be the encouragement Gary

needed. He glanced in her eyes and then said, "Yeah, I'm scared to talk. I don't know where to start. Damn— I'm all confused—but I've got to talk to somebody!"

At this Mrs. Alvarez told him that he had just now used books as a screen between the two of them. "I've worried sometimes that your novels and your fantasies are a screen between you and other people, especially people your own age."

As the conversation continued, little by little Gary mentioned his difficult relationships with other boys, his fear of girls, his feelings of loneliness and "all that crap." At the end of the period he asked to come back to talk more about "all this garbage," and they agreed on a time the following week.

Mrs. Alvarez was exhilarated at this turn in their conversation. She hoped to be able to continue the interviews during the remaining two months of the school year. But on the morning of the next session, she received a message from Gary: "I can't make it today. Anyway, maybe we ought to drop our last topic of conversation. See you in class." The rejection stung Mrs. Alvarez. For several weeks Gary avoided her, and then when he did drop in again, he was armed with a new short story and a whole file of literary questions. Mrs. Alvarez had taken a risk and failed. Gary graduated, a talented writer and critic, but a lonely, distant young man.

*   *   *

There will undoubtedly be times when you the counselor will attempt to determine which personal revelations are likely to frighten the client away from the counseling relationship. This temptation is difficult to avoid after someone has abruptly ended a relationship that appeared to be both healthy and helpful. Only experience will demonstrate to you that planning responses will not decrease the number of "failures" you will experience in your attempts to relate humanly to those who come to you for help. More often than not it is the risk that is personally frightening that will permit you to break through protective defenses and begin relating personally with the client who so clearly needs human contact.

Bill, a young and promising member of an investment firm, brought his growing depression, fears, and resentments to a counseling psychologist. In the first session Bill described his periods of depression. And then without pause, he launched into a long account of his family history. He described his parents, his two sisters, the family financial circumstances, the cities where they had lived while he was growing up. When he spoke of his father, he became vehement and soon focused his story on his father's attempts to dominate him. "Like the time I was nine years old, and I wanted to play football, my father . . .," and he related in detail an incident from his childhood. He felt sure, he said, that his father's domineering attitudes were at the root of his depression. For nearly half the counseling session, Bill talked on, quickly and smoothly, without stopping for a comment from the counselor. Occasionally he glanced in the counselor's direction but he never looked into his eyes.

Soon the counselor realized that Bill would probably talk uninterruptedly for the entire hour. He might as well have been talking into a tape recorder. The other human being in the room seemed reduced by Bill into an absorbing ear. His story was, moreover, boring in its details and in its relentless progress. The counselor was experiencing by this time both boredom and anger because he felt that Bill had erased him.

At this point, if the counselor had overlooked his own feelings, he could have focused his attention on what Bill was saying about the father-son relationship. Or, as Bill's story continued, he could have interrupted with questions or comments. But instead he let himself feel and express his here-and-now emotions. Becoming very human, he interrupted Bill and said, "I feel that you are completely ignoring me. I might as well be a tape recorder. I don't seem to make any difference to you, and I'm getting a little upset. Would it matter to you at all if I just turned on the recorder and left the room?"

Stopped for the moment, Bill apologized and said the counselor did make a difference. But then he immediately returned to his story. The counselor interrupted again; Bill apologized again, shifted his position more in the direction of the counselor, but once more plunged into his story. He seemed incapable of hearing what was being said to him. Finally the counselor said, "I am bored with your long story. I don't like being ignored, and I'm getting angrier by the minute because you don't seem to hear me when I ask you to notice me. Now, either you talk to me and let me be a part of this conversation or we end the counseling right now."

This time Bill did stop. He was visibly bewildered and embarrassed. His face grew red. After a few moments of stunned silence, he spoke but in a changed tone of voice. "Nobody ever said that to me before." Although there was a trace of anger, his whole manner and tone expressed the shock of unwelcome discovery.

The rest of the interview took a new direction. Bill and the counselor dealt with what was happening between them. Then Bill admitted that he probably did not pay much attention to any person he was talking to. As the conversation continued, Bill recognized that many people during their talks with him simply fell silent and later made some excuse to leave. "Nobody ever said to me what you just did. Nobody ever said 'you're ignoring me.' But I was ignoring them, and they must have felt it. I have noticed that as soon as there's some break in my talk, people leave."

For the rest of that interview and in later sessions, Bill and the counselor for the most part kept their attention on what was going on between them and on what Bill was actually feeling, not on what he had felt as a child with his father. This focus proved very difficult for Bill, but thanks to it he was able to identify and express such things as his desire to be liked and his realization that few people did like him. The counselor's honest and personal reactions to him became important and instructive. The relationship between the two men became Bill's first successful adult friendship. Because in that first interview the counselor had reacted humanly, all the later sessions took a direction that led Bill closer to himself and to the real roots of his depressions, fears, and resentments.

2. Human Communication

Impersonal Communication

In order to avoid impersonal communication with the person asking your help, it is important that you "stay in the room"—that you remain aware of what is happening here and now in you and in the other person, and that you respond to these present events. Why?

As we have said repeatedly, the relationship between you and the person coming to you for help is, in our opinion, central to the success of the counseling. You and another human being are contacting each other. For both of you the contact is full of risks, obstacles, pitfalls. Both of you may fear that contact even as you desire it. The person before you has probably found contact with others frightening, disappointing, perhaps nearly impossible. When he met you and during your first contact, he sensed your willingness to communicate with him, and he decided that human contact was worth one more try.

All his problems are present in him, and they will

appear in his relationship with you just as they appear in
his everyday world. He will tend to hear you as he hears
others, respond to you as he responds to others, ignore
you as he ignores others, impose upon you as he imposes
upon others, hide from you as he hides from others. In
the here and now of your conversation with him, the
person in all his confusions will be revealed; at the same
time, he will be changing either in terms of growth or
deterioration. Either his relationship with you will,
thanks to your assistance, begin to differ from his other
relationships and he, too, will begin to change for the
better, or his relationship with you will remain a pure
repetition and become just another situation where his
difficulties remain unaltered. Our point here is this: the
here and now fluctuations and qualities of your relationship during the actual conversations between you will be
to a major degree the actual healing and growth you seek
for in the counseling. If this is so, it seems most important that during all the counseling conversations, you
"stay in the room."

By staying in the room we mean that you remain
attentive to what is happening here and now in you, in
the other person, and between the two of you. This
means that you remain aware of your own present, actual
feelings. This means trying not to repress feelings or to
be deceitful in expressing yourself. It means setting aside
insincerity even when insincerity seems the more human-
itarian way.

Staying in the room means being genuinely interested
in the other person and allowing yourself at this moment
to enter his world. It means helping him to remain in the
present with his real feelings and his real reactions to

you. It means also remaining attentive to all his forms of communication, verbal and non-verbal.

Deceiving for the Sake of Helping

Perhaps it is helpful to look first at the impersonal form of communication: how might you "leave the room"? One of the easiest ways to leave the room is to deceive for the sake of helping. For example, you may find yourself, in your anxiety to help this person, feigning interest in his rambling when, in reality, you are disturbed or bored by it. Surely, you think, admitting your real feelings would disappoint and hurt the person. But such feigning, even when it seems in the best interests of the client, introduces pretense into your relationship with him, and, as in close relationships, the person will probably sense that pretense. If he senses insincerity, then he will be disappointed and hurt. What he needs most is precisely sincerity even when it does bring discomfort, and even if it risks breaking off the relationship. For what good is it to this person to enter one more polite, façade-ridden friendship? By leaving aside your real feelings, you have not helped but hindered.

You may "leave the room" by deceiving in still another way. A client may say, "Remember what I told you two weeks ago about my argument with my father?" You may not remember; or you may recall only that the story was tedious. You might feign a little and say, "Yes, I remember. Go on." But the client's question may have been precisely an unconscious feeler to find out if you are really interested in him. Again sensing the insincerity in your response, he may conclude that you are not really interested. You just want to get on with the conversation. It would seem better for the development of the relationship if you were honest: "No, I don't remember." Or, "All I remember is that the story was long!" Perhaps a mutual smile will follow and help put the client at ease. But above all, he will sense that you would never have said anything so threatening to your own reputation and to the counseling relationship unless it were the truth. He senses, then, that you are honest with him, and are letting him make contact with your real self. He can trust you. You are right there with him, and really interested. He has a friend.

Another tempting form of pretense that will drive the conversation to the impersonal level is this: you may pretend to have an illuminating understanding of the other person and his problem when, in reality, you are bewildered and unsure. Needing to protect yourself and to maintain a superiority, you may by your look or by nods or by words indicate that you have placed everything in its proper light, and have the penetrating insight that will lead to a happy solution. Needless to say, such feigning removes you immediately from the realities of the here and now in the room—from your own feelings, from the other person's real needs, and from his responses.

Sometimes the deceit takes another direction: you deceive yourself. You may assume that because you have heard of similar "cases," you can classify the client, and see his problem as, for instance, "the usual parent-child conflict." Thinking that you understand, you no longer attend to this person as this individual nor to the details of his conversations as really unique. Perhaps as you

recall your own experience with the "parent-child conflict," you project your own past feelings and attitudes
onto the other person. You no longer hear him. You
have "left the room."

Curiosity and Impatience

Another way to yield to impersonal communication is to
let curiosity overcome you. In his conversation with you,
the other person may bring up material which interests
you for reasons other than the counseling. Wanting to
know more, you may question the client in a way that
leads both of you away from the real issues. For example, a teenage girl, seeking help from a school counselor,
may talk about her sexual activity with a "boy here at
school." The counselor, thinking he knows who the boy
is, may out of curiosity ask his name or, by innuendo,
seek clues to his identity. Such questioning may disturb
the girl and cause her to wonder if the counselor is trustworthy. Is he going to tell others? Will it "get back" to
the boy that she is taking her problems to a counselor?
Another example: in talking to a man seeking her help,
a woman counselor may attempt to discover if she is
attractive to men; or a male counselor may attempt to
exhibit masculine appeal when he is with a female client,
just to see if he is capable of effecting a response. A
teacher, approached by a student for counseling, may ask
leading questions to discover if the student considers him
a good teacher. A secretary whom others seek out for
lunch-hour counseling may try to find out if a certain
person in the office holds a grudge against her or has
gossiped about her. If you were to give in to such curi-

osity about factors unrelated to the client's present needs
and to the here-and-now relationship between you, you
could lessen the person's trust in you, cause him to feel
"used," and you could lead yourself away from the
present interaction. By giving in to irrelevant curiosity,
you "leave the room."

Finally, you may "leave the room" by becoming impatient. Anxious to get at the problem and answer it,
you may address all your attention to the apparent question before knowing if it is indeed the real one. The
person's apparent problem may be whether or not to
change jobs, change courses in school, change doctors,
change a will. The more fundamental problem may be
the person's inability to be himself in the presence of
others, his failure in human relationships, his fear of his
own tendencies. Perhaps the real problem is the client's
inability to make a decision on his own. The very need to
ask advice might indicate that this person depends too
much on what a parent or a spouse or an employer thinks.
To center on the change of jobs or the change of classes
is to overlook this person's real need.

Sometimes, of course, the person may help you to
avoid the real question because he himself does not know
what it is. Often enough, though, the client does know
that the first problem he brings to you is just a decoy
problem, a symptom of more fundamental difficulties, an
immediate conflict with roots far deeper in his personality than he is able to express. Perhaps he can name his
more fundamental conflicts but is ashamed to speak of
them. He wants you to help him bring these conflicts to
expression. He wants you to go beyond the difficulty he
says is bothering him. He does not want you to spend

the conversation discussing job possibilities or types of school courses. If you, impatient to bring help to this person, address yourself primarily to the problems as he first states them, you may be leaving the room and leaving behind a person disappointed and unsatisfied.

Personal Communication

On the positive side, the key to achieving personal communication with another human being will be your sincere interest in him, plus your ability and willingness to enter his world. If these attitudes are not in you, it is better to tell the client that you do not think you are the one to help him. For pretended interest or pretended sympathy with his viewpoints can only injure the human relationship between the two of you. If this relationship cannot be genuine, fruitful counseling may prove impossible.

There are many ways to allow your interest in this person to develop naturally, as you remain present to his here and now reality in the room. Here is a human being who somehow likes you and trusts you, and who at some level of his personality wants to reveal himself to you. As he sits here with you, he is probably alive with emotion, whether or not those emotions are consciously felt or accepted. His history, his background, his conflicts, his buried feelings, his trust and mistrust are here in your presence, groping for articulation, understanding, and acceptance. This person is a rich world opening to your gaze and concern. Despite the fears and threats you may experience, allow yourself to look upon that world and enter it. Allow this person to lead you into his framework of meanings and values, his way of interpreting the world, his way of responding to his universe. Some clients may lead you into a world of fear, confusion, and conflicting value-frameworks. Others may invite you to share their viewpoint which may differ dramatically from your own. Whatever the client's world, entering it is an adventure. Allow yourself to find what is fascinating in this person. If such a spirit can be in you, then you are developing in the here and now a human and healing relationship with this person. Probably few persons in the client's whole experience have cared enough to enter his world with a spirit of interest and acceptance. Even those who protest love for him may have thought that their love forced them to shut out and condemn what the client values most. Finding a friend willing to experience his viewpoints and values without censure can be of maximum importance to this person's development. You communicate personally, then, when you allow yourself to be sincerely interested in this person and when you allow yourself, despite fears and threats, to enter his world as he reveals it to you in the here and now.

Attending to All Forms of Communication

Communicating personally with this person, entering his world with interest and acceptance, means that you remain alert to all forms of communication from him. He will speak to you with words, and he will speak to you without words. Both forms are important.

First of all, his verbal communication. He may, for

example, tell you a story about himself. Where does the story start? Why did he choose this story? Who is in it? What does the client seem to find in this story? What is the story really about? Is the story important in itself? Is it important to this person? Does he seem really interested in it himself? Is it an invitation to you to probe further? Is it a smoke screen to hide his real feelings? Is it an introduction to something else? Do you find it interesting or boring? Does the length and manner of telling indicate that this person is a compulsive talker? Or that he has no one to talk to in his time of confusion or crisis? Is he pleading or fighting with you?

Perhaps he tells you his views on life or his opinions about how things ought to be. He may describe his moral values, the principles he tries to incorporate into his living. Such statements can give an important insight into this person. What is it he claims to value? Are these values in conflict with his emotions or his activities? Does he really believe what he is saying? Has he imported these values from others without appropriating them for himself? Is he defending these principles or deprecating them? Why? Do his words tell you that he considers these principles or values certain and irrefutable? Does he defend these views in a manner that indicates fear and insecurity about them? Although the words themselves may not really express what is in the client, the very fact that he wants to tell you these things, and in this way, can be very important. The very contrast of the words with the reality can prove helpful.

Does he speak personally or impersonally? Does he make broad generalizations instead of speaking of himself directly? Does he speak of his own emotions, of his

own ideas, *as his own,* or does he express them in impersonal ways, such as, "There ought to be," or "A lot of
people think," or "Everybody does it this way," or
"Everybody gets angry when," or "You've got to fight
back when," or "A guy really has to watch out when."
Often if the client does not speak in a personal way,
owning to his feelings as his own, you have a tip-off that
he himself does not realize that these feelings are in him.
He may be unaware of these feelings even though they
are exerting strong pressure on him. He may be so
distant from himself that he does not quite know what it
means to have any feeling at all even though at the
moment he is a mass of tensions and functional disorders.

Sometimes speaking impersonally is a way of self-
protection. If the client can say, "Everybody feels this
way," or "In our society people are always doing this,"
he has not said that *he* feels or thinks this way; and so
he has talked to you without definitely revealing to you
his own inner self. Fear of embarrassment or rejection
may keep him from clear revelation of this inner and
often "shameful" self. Generalities provide protection.

If the client speaks impersonally of his own emotions,
he may be indicating his dependence upon the opinions
of others. Perhaps he measures his worth by what he
thinks others think of him. Or perhaps he looks to others
to determine what his standards should be. He may find
his values in the codes or rules or judgments of his parents, his spouse, his employers, his sports club, his social
group, his church, his political party, his local community.
By speaking impersonally he is expressing his values in
the way that he holds them—from the outside, not from
his own conscious understanding and appropriation.

If for whatever reason the client speaks in impersonal ways, he is revealing much of himself to you. He is telling you that he is distant from himself. He is either not recognizing or not expressing his own feelings. And until he is able to recognize, accept, and express these feelings, he will remain in confusion and distress. You may need to show much understanding, patience, and acceptance before this person can at some point begin to speak of his feelings as his own. It is seldom easy for someone accustomed to impersonal expressions to admit that his fears are his fears, his shames are his shames, his desires are his desires, and not those of a protecting group. It may be extremely difficult for him to accept the fact that he allows others to dictate how he should feel, judge, and react. When he begins to come closer to his own feelings, he will probably let you know by using phrases such as "I feel" in the place of "everybody thinks."

More on Verbal Communication

Sometimes the client will abruptly change the subject; here, too, is a form of "verbal communication." Perhaps the conversation was coming too close to something he wants to hide or cannot bring himself to talk about. He may be ashamed to discuss what the conversation was leading to. Perhaps he wants to avoid speaking of something which he thinks might make you dislike him. He may fear you will condemn something he holds dear but feels guilty about. If he continues to talk on a certain topic, he may feel forced to examine what he clings to but fears to look at. For these and many other reasons, the client may suddenly switch to a new topic of conversation.

If you are wondering why he changed the subject, it seems well to tell him so, and in this way, to help him come closer to what is so bothersome.

Here is an example of a client's changing the subject in a significant way. A forty-five-year-old woman who prided herself on her liberal opinions and her popularity with young people came to realize during counseling sessions that, in contrast to her views of freedom for everyone, she habitually forced her opinions and decisions on other people. She thought she knew "what was good for them," and tried her best to make others see and accept her views of their lives. Just discovering that she had such habits of manipulating shocked the woman. Her activities were in opposition to what she held theoretically: she was dominating people at the very moment she was defending their freedom to make their own decisions. After she had realized what she was doing, she continued to find it hard to discuss her manipulating tendencies with the counselor. Whenever she sensed that the conversation might lead to a discussion of them, she adroitly switched the topic to something else. The counselor, alert to what was happening, each time expressed concern over this change of topic. And each time, with much pain, the woman admitted her fear of discussing her "hideous self—me, the manipulator." Yet, with each discussion of this repugnant part of her, she came closer to accepting it and dealing with it in her daily contacts with others.

Sometimes "verbal" communication will take the form of the client's ignoring your question and answering another. Here, too, he may be telling you that he fears to explore or to reveal himself in a direct answer. So he attempts to divert your questioning into a less painful channel. Sometimes, of course, he may be letting you know that he does not listen to you, that he cannot hear what you and perhaps most other people say to him. For whatever reason he ignores your question, it seems well that you tell him your wonder and concern about his response.

Sometimes a client's verbal communication will, by its length and disorder, tell you much about this person. He may without stopping narrate several incidents or stories which have only loose, if any, connection. He seems to jump from event to event. When he speaks this way, he may be revealing how disorganized his own thoughts and feelings are. He himself is lost in a maze of events and emotions, all of which make demands on him. He doesn't know where he is. When he attempts to communicate about his world, he must jump from event to event and from emotion to emotion. Here, you the counselor can help by pointing out that his breathless narrations may be revealing inner chaos. For, despite the power of his conflicting emotions, the client may never have interpreted his need to tell long, detailed jumbles of events as an articulation of his own inner confusion. But when he hears you tell him what you hear through his words, he will often recognize the truth. "You're right—that's the way my mind is going all the time. I am all confused."

In such a situation it helps to ask the client to compose one brief sentence which sums up what he has said. "In one sentence, what do you consider the point of all this?" Or, you may ask him to select just one or two adjectives which best describe his emotions at the moment. The verbal discipline can help him sort out his thoughts and pull his feelings together. You may have to continue to stop him in his stories and ask him to sum up or to state briefly how he feels. The client may find this discipline difficult, but he will usually begin to use it as a structure for organization; the continued discipline helps him pick out what is most real in the jumble—and it reduces the jumbles. It gives him some sense of order. At times you may have to do the summing-up for him because he is so lost in his own disorder.

Sometimes a long story is merely a defense or a plea for approval. The client, often unconsciously, feels that he must explain fully why he feels as he does or why he reacted as he did. He tells in detail about an encounter with another person. He explains carefully why he answered in such a way or why he changed the subject or did not accept the invitation. When such stories go on and on, you the counselor can point out what you think is behind the narration. "I feel you have to defend yourself by showing me why you spoke as you did to your friend." Or, "I think you are trying to win my approval for what you did." It may take time before the client can admit to himself what he is doing; but his detailed story often does prove how unsure he feels and how much he looks to others for approval and direction.

Sometimes a deep and sincere emotion will appear only briefly in a long story. Having said something with marked feeling, the person quickly continues to the next part of the story. Although he may have for a moment been ready to cry or ready to explode, he passes over the feeling and brings up something new. For example, in a long description of events, the person may slip in the sentence, "I know what I really need," and then go on immediately to describe another situation. When he spoke the sentence, his whole body responded. Sometimes "I get furious" slips in among the incidents and gets lost again. But at the moment of saying those words, the person's demeanor changed. If you pick up those short cues, you can help the client discover and admit his own feelings. Stop the story and ask him to repeat the statement which he quickly passed over despite the fact that his whole being had responded with feeling. Ask him to repeat "I need love" or "I get furious" or "I feel like screaming." Or, point out the emotion you noticed as he described some incident. Often as he repeats the sentence or hears what you noticed, he does discern the emotion more clearly. Sometimes the repetition helps him face an emotion he knew he had but wanted to run from. Usually your focusing on the emotional sentence will reveal a deep and central problem which was getting lost among the stories.

Sometimes the person's verbal communication indirectly reveals his fears. For example, David, a college freshman from a strict religious background, was shocked during his humanities seminar to find students from a similar background departing from the strict sexual and doctrinal norms he knew they had been taught. For weeks during the seminar, he stoutly defended traditional principles in the face of criticism and ridicule from his classmates. Finally he came to the seminar leader, Miss Hall, for help. He kept repeating during their conversations that "The guys are really hurting themselves when they talk that way (against traditional mores), and I want to help them. I want to convince them that they are wrong—for their own sakes I want to convince them." While David talked this way about his classmates, Miss Hall seemed to hear behind these words some unexpressed sentences. David seemed to be saying, "My whole world structure is shaken by these students. They are destroying my neat, secure, all-inclusive world of certitudes and guidelines. Stop them! Also, I feel responsible for the whole world. I've got to convert others, show them the true path, keep them from error and sin, or else they—and I—may be eternally punished." David's choosing to discuss his classmates was his way of crying out for help with his own internal world.

Miss Hall told David what she felt was coming through his words. She told him that she thought he was afraid to have his world shaken, his certitudes questioned; and at the same time, he felt he had to convert and save the other students. Although at first disturbed by what Miss Hall said, David began visibly to "melt" and to admit that he was terribly afraid his structured universe was really vulnerable. "I didn't know that that was what I was feeling, but now I know, at least I think I know."

As the informal after-class conversations continued during the following weeks, David began more and more to accept his own confusion and to realize that it was possible for him to live constructively and religiously without having irrefutable certitudes, and that he was not responsible for the conversion of the world. As a result of these conversations with Miss Hall, David's honesty about his feelings of confusion and fear became a catalyst for honesty and self-discovery among other members of the seminar.

Non-Verbal Communication

Beyond the client's words are communications which
demand that you not so much hear as "see" what is
being said. You communicate personally with this person
when you remain alert to all these non-verbal communications. He probably communicates much the same thing
to other people, and now you in this room have the opportunity to do what probably few persons have done:
you can accept, understand, and respond to these unspoken communications.

Many things are speaking to you: the way this person
is dressed, the condition of his complexion, where he
sits, if he chooses his chair or waits for directions from
you, how he sits, constrictions in his shoulders, hands,
knees, the direction and intensity of his gaze, nervous
twitches, hand or foot movements, coughing, throat
clearing, frequent face-touching. His gaze is important.
If during most of the conversation he will not look into
your eyes, he is perhaps signaling his fear of discovery,
a sense of shame, a fear of disapproval, a great shyness
and fear of other people. You may find it helpful to
mention to him your wonder about his avoiding your
eyes. Although your statement may have nothing to do
with the story he is telling you, it may have everything
to do with this person's human relationships. Right now
is the time to face this difficulty as it appears in the
human relationship between the two of you.

Sometimes you may notice a marked discrepancy between the person's words and his non-verbal communications. For example, although his words are pleasant
enough and the topic neutral, his tone of voice, his

posture, and his facial expression may be displaying an unacknowledged anger at you. Or the discrepancy may be the opposite: while he tells you about his anger at someone, he continues to smile or keeps an even voice tone. Perhaps while he discusses a certain person, his voice tone remains the same, but he rings his hands or twists a scrap of paper into contorted shapes. Perhaps he may smile pleasantly during the entire interview despite the fact that he is telling you how depressed he is and how close he is to suicide. All these discrepancies between verbal and non-verbal messages, all the tones, body movements, facial expressions are addressing you. As human counselor, interested in what is happening here and now in the room, you will want to recognize these communications, accept them, and respond honestly to them.

When, for example, these non-verbal communications are not in keeping with the client's words, he may be revealing that he does not realize what his emotions are, or that he is ashamed of them, or that he fears them, or that for any number of reasons he cannot accept them as his own. He is deliberately or indeliberately blotting something of himself out of his awareness. Or perhaps guilt and self-punishment keep him from full expression of anger or hatred or self-pity. He can talk of these emotions, acknowledge that he has them, but not let himself feel or express them. He may, for instance, consider it wrong to hate his mother and therefore, when he speaks of what she has done to him, he continues to smile. Owning to hate, or allowing himself to feel it with freedom, threatens him too much. Perhaps he is angry with you, but he forbids himself to admit or express such anger because you, after all, are trying to help him and are his friend. And so in the counseling conversation, as in his everyday life, there is a discrepancy between his verbal and non-verbal communications. In his ordinary life he probably tries to cover up, both for his own sake and for others, any expression of unpopular or uncomfortable emotions, such as anger, aversion, disapproval or hatred. He may think that he must under all circumstances remain cheerful and pleasant despite any other feelings he might be experiencing.

If you remain in the room with him and accept all these non-verbal communications, you may say to him what he needs most to hear and what perhaps no one else has ever said to him despite the fact that he has acted non-verbally with them just as he is acting now with you. You may tell him that you sense, despite all he is saying, that he is angry with you. You may express your own wonder that he can speak calmly of his mother while at the same time he is crushing and kneading his empty cigarette pack. You may point out that you wish he would look at you, and that you wonder if he is afraid or ashamed to. It is quite possible that your addressing yourself to his significant non-verbal communications may be the way to reach this person at the level where his concern really lies.

Success

All the while you communicate personally with this person, the relationship between you two is undergoing changes. You are changing in response to him, and he is changing in response to you. The relationship itself is developing. If you allow yourself to communicate honestly, aware of your responses and willing to share these very human responses with this person, then this relationship can develop in a way most helpful to the counseling. As we mentioned before, this person's real problems often center in his human relationships. Something is awry there; he cannot respond as he wishes to other people, and they do not respond to him in the way he longs for. Yet, he does not know for sure why things are amiss; or, if he thinks he knows why, he does not feel able to alter the situation alone. If you can enter into a human relationship with him here and now in the counseling room, many characteristics of his other relationships will appear. You will probably experience many of the same reactions that others experience when they are with this person at home or at work or at school or at a social engagement. You may experience boredom, fear, aversion, attraction, confusion, frustration, affection, anger, or a combination of these or other emotions. As human counselor, you remain aware of these varying reactions in yourself, and then attempt honestly to share them with the client. You may tell him that you are attracted to him, and yet are repelled by his barrage of words and his swagger. You may express your frustration in trying to reach him because he never seems to hear. You may tell him that his whining and complaining makes you uncomfortable and causes you to wonder if he does not indulge in excessive self-pity. You may tell him that, while you admire him, you feel "taken in" by him, "had," and that, therefore, you are tempted to withdraw from further contact with him. You may tell him that you feel tenderness for him and wish that he would not condemn and cover up the softer, gentler, more appealing part of himself which is in some way, probably non-verbally, coming through to you. You may tell him that you sense a fear in him, a fear of you, or of possible sexual or hostile feelings toward you. This list of expressions is endless because each relationship has its own variations and shadings of emotion. The point is this: you, as a human being, allow yourself to feel and to respond humanly, and you share as honestly as possible with the other person the nature and quality of these reactions. In this way you do, in a most important manner, communicate yourself.

Why is all this personal communication significant? It is significant because, as we have said before, the counseling relationship is a human relationship and is, therefore, repeating patterns found in the other human relationships which the client shares in. As we have mentioned, you are probably feeling what many people have felt toward this person. For example, you may be experiencing a combination of attraction and repulsion, frustration and concern. But when others have felt these reactions, they have been afraid to tell this person about them. They have feared to express what they are feeling. They have instead perhaps made excuses to leave or found reasons for not accepting further invitations. They have gone to another table during the lunch hour or arranged to take a coffee break at another time.

As you are talking with this person and feeling similar emotions, you, too, are probably afraid to tell him what you feel. Whether the emotion is tenderness or aversion, it remains risky to express it; and you will probably share the fear others have experienced in similar circumstances. Yet, if you are the human counselor, you will want to take the risk, to act in spite of your fear. You, unlike many others in the client's life, are willing to take the risk of telling him what your real responses are. Perhaps no one has ever told him these things before. Or, if they have, they have done so in a way the client cannot hear. When you say them, he can accept them because he senses that you do care about him and accept him. Only when that concern is real, have you in the first place consented to enter into the counseling relationship. The person, sensing your human care and acceptance, has probably already experienced an inner peace, a freedom and openness to you. With you it is all right to admit to failings. You will like him anyway. In addition, as you express your honest reactions, the person can sense how solid and real your relationship is. Rejoicing, perhaps unconsciously, in the fact that he has entered a real, sincere, concerned human relationship, he can experience an acceptance of himself, a satisfaction with himself that can free him to hear what you are saying. You may, in fact, be telling him something his marriage partner or his parents or his fellow workers have been trying to get across to him, but ineffectually because they have cloaked their words in vagueness, in innuendo, in ambiguous references, well-meant but unclear. Or perhaps their belligerent tone or obvious lack of understanding when they attempted to tell him "what he needed to know" signaled to him that they really did not care; his response was self-defense. But more commonly the client has never heard from anyone what you are saying. You have expressed what his marriage partner or his fellow workers have felt but never expressed. You have expressed what his acquaintances feel but never mention either out of fear of incurring the person's anger or simply out of lack of interest in him. Obviously such communication does ask that you accept your own humanity, that you allow yourself to enter a human relationship with the client, that you remain aware of your own responses, that you care about the client, that you enter his world and try to experience it with understanding and acceptance, that you share with him your real reactions to him, that you have courage to risk his anger, his condemnation of you, his severing the relationship, his threatening your professional career. The response you hope for is worth all this. You hope that this person, in the room with you, will begin to work through a human relationship in a new way, a way more honest, open, and humanly successful than any other he has tried. You hope that he will experience what it is to touch and be touched by another. You have modeled for him what a real friend can be—interested, honest, sincere, unafraid to experience many emotions and to express them. He senses that it is possible to be all of himself, negative and positive, when he is with others without receiving in return their condemnation. For he does not condemn you in his deepest self; he is glad for your honesty and feels that you have cared enough to share yourself with him. He now has all the more encouragement to be honest both with himself and with you, and therefore to develop with you an even stronger and more satisfactory human relationship. Such is the response you hope for. Although his initial reaction to your honesty may be hostile, he is probably sensing within himself those elements which

lead him finally to accept both himself and you, and to
enter more deeply into this one honest, human relationship. Your hope beyond this hope is that having once
experienced such a relationship, he will find that something natural within him has been released; and the direction of all his other relationships will henceforth tend
to be positive.

Failure

Communicating personally with the person asking your
help does not always have happy results. If you express
your here-and-now feelings, and respond to all forms
of communication, you may offend, frighten, embarrass,
or anger the other person. He may resent you as an
intruder, or as one who makes him say what he does
not want to say. He may hotly deny the emotions you
say you sense in him. And for any such reason he may
end the counseling. If he leaves you, you will perhaps
have to deal with your own sense of failure, and you
will probably be tempted not to be so aware and open
the next time. The risks are real and sometimes seem
too great. If you continue to try to "stay in the room"
with persons seeking help, chances are you will at some
time offend and will cause the end of the counseling.
You will risk and lose. A lawyer who responds to his
client's nervous gestures and high-pitched laugh may
find himself considered an intruder, and no longer this
man's lawyer. A nurse being honest with a patient who
has sought her help may find herself reported to the
authorities. A man in open conversation with a friend
seeking help may find that he has alienated this friend,

and will no longer be asked to play golf with him or meet him for lunch. The risk is real and asks courage and perseverance in the face of occasional failure.

Sometimes, too, if you "stay in the room" by expressing your feelings and by responding to various forms of communication, you may find that you are simply wrong. You have misread this communication; you have reacted to something not there in this person. Often the other person will stay with you and help you see better what is happening in him; but sometimes he will be offended and disappointed in you. He may withdraw more and more, and if he continues the conversations with you, he may attempt to over-defend himself or to deceive you.

Mr. McKay was teaching a freshman psychology class which included a weekly period of group encounter. During the first weeks of the class, he noticed that Terry, a well-built, very tall lad, seemed to be the center of whispered conversations during the lectures; and yet in the encounter group, he said nothing. He seemed to hang back and be scowling at the proceedings. Finally Mr. McKay, incensed at this behavior, confronted Terry. He told him he thought he was heckling the class during the lecture times but was afraid to say anything in the group when commentary was welcome. Mr. McKay expressed irritation and scorn. Terry looked bewildered and merely mumbled a few words. After the class, two other students came to Mr. McKay and said, "You're all wrong about Terry. He's a great guy but very shy. He's scared to death he's going to fail and can't make himself talk up in class. He never talks much." As it turned out, others were questioning Terry during the lecture class and he, embarrassed, answered them, but never originated these undercover conversations. Others spoke to him because they felt for him and wanted to help him overcome his shyness. Mr. McKay learned later from Terry himself that the lad was on an athletic scholarship which he would lose if he failed. His own large body, with its power to physically overwhelm anyone, greatly increased his shyness. He was actually afraid of overpowering or hurting another unintentionally. During most of the semester, despite Mr. McKay's public apology to him in class, Terry remained reserved and silent.

Examples

We will now consider two examples of individual counseling which illustrate how personal communication was, for the most part, helpful.

A Catholic priest called Jim came on the recommendation of others to a psychologist, Dr. Hanson. At first Jim found it hard to agree to scheduled meetings and the usual fees because then he would seem to be needing "psychological help." "All I want," he said, "is someone to talk to, and my friends said you would be a good one to come to." Finally, after some conversation, Jim agreed to come for conversations under the usual arrangements.

After they had reached an agreement on a time schedule, Dr. Hanson told Jim of his own background—that he, too, had served as a clergyman; he was an ordained Lutheran minister but did not now function as such. Jim said he felt at once more at home because he would not have to go into long explanations of those problems which arose because he was in the ministry. But during their third conversation, Dr. Hanson noticed that as Jim related an event from the past week, he was in non-verbal ways exhibiting anger and aversion toward the counselor. Although he was describing a successful encounter, the priest's shoulders, arms, and hands were taut, his eyes angry, and his voice tones strong and sharp. When Jim paused, Dr. Hanson said, "I have the feeling that you are angry with me."

At first Jim ignored the remark and tried to switch back to his story. But then, after a pause, he faced Dr. Hanson squarely and burst into a controlled but real tirade. "I'm mad because you are a minister!" He expressed his aversion for anyone officially connected with an institutional church. As he continued to talk with his controlled but genuine anger, he said, "You make me mad for other reasons. I'm really jealous of you—yes, jealous." He said he was jealous because Dr. Hanson, who had once suffered through problems like his own, now possessed academic degrees, was happily married, and was successful in a profession unconnected with the church. As he spoke, streams of hostility and longing came forth; Jim directed them to whole groups of men and situations.

Although Jim's story up to then had included nothing about his relationship with the psychologist, the most significant part of the early counseling was precisely what was happening between him and Dr. Hanson. Yet Jim was not even allowing himself to realize the emotions he was experiencing right there in the room. Dr. Hanson, on the other hand, noticed the non-verbal communication, sensed Jim's anger, and concluded that the anger was directed at the psychologist himself. At the same time he recognized his own fear of telling Jim about the anger. He did not want to offend nor did he welcome a blast of anger at himself. But aware of the importance of their relationship, and aware of the importance of honestly sharing his own feelings, Dr. Hanson took the risk and expressed his own human response to what was happening in the room. Thanks to that expression, Jim was able to own up to hostilities, desires, fears, and jealousies which had in the first place brought him to the counselor for help. The hostility and jealousy Jim felt toward Dr. Hanson was only an instance of emotions which were deeply troubling him. By "staying in the room" with the non-verbal communications and with his own feelings, Dr. Hanson had helped give the counseling a new and more fruitful direction.

* * *

On the recommendation of a friend, Harry Kozad telephoned a counselor, Ruth Friedman. "Last week," he said, "my wife locked me out of the house, and she hasn't given in. I don't understand. We never have fights; we've never quarreled; I've been faithful—the whole bit. But now all of a sudden she says she's beginning divorce proceedings. I talked to her today, and she says she'll come to talk to you if she can come by herself. I suppose I'd better see you, too." Ruth agreed to see the Kozads separately, as they wished.

Mrs. Kozad came first. She was a young woman, married two years to the young insurance executive. She confirmed the fact that she and her husband never quarreled or fought. There had been a growing tension between them, but it found expression only in long evening silences and sexual coldness. "Twice I suggested that we get some advice from somebody, but Harry said he couldn't see why. But he must have known something was wrong. He's just too proud to admit it. That's why I finally had to lock him out."

While she said these things, Mrs. Kozad remained composed and pleasant. There was little trace of anger in her voice. Then she began to tell Ruth about the many situations in which her husband had caused her days of worry, had neglected her, had been cold and distant, and in other ways had, as she said, "made me furious." "I was boiling inside most of the time. I was losing sleep, yet he wouldn't admit anything was wrong." While she was relating these situations and telling how angry she had been, Mrs. Kozad kept her voice even and her face composed.

Ruth, noticing the discrepancy and bothered by it, mentioned it to the woman. After a short and embarrassed exchange, Mrs. Kozad did admit that she had trained herself never to show anger. She did not want to be known as a "nag" or a "shrew." "I have always despised anyone who lost their temper. My mother taught me always to control myself." She said she never displayed anger at Harry; instead she let him know her upset by remarks she strategically placed in their conversations. "Yet he never seems to get the point."

Ruth told Mrs. Kozad how much she herself, the counselor, was disturbed by the calmness. "And I have felt during this conversation that you have been trying to impress me with your calmness. I am not impressed, but disturbed. I think I would really be upset if you began dropping hints and making well-placed insinuations instead of telling me outright what was going on in you, and what you wanted to say."

Ruth's reactions led to a discussion of the reaction Mr. Kozad may have had when his wife remained calm on the outside while dropping hints and making insinuations of displeasure. Perhaps Mr. Kozad had felt the same disturbance but, for some reason or other, had never spoken of his emotions to his wife. Perhaps he, too, had felt annoyed and angry; but instead of expressing his anger, he had simply changed the subject or become silent while he hid his exasperation and frustration.

Later in the conversation, Mrs. Kozad talked about her husband's coming home late in the evening. Once more, her voice and demeanor displayed no anger; but as she spoke, she began to wring her hands. She said she thought her husband was devoting too much time to his work and not enough time to her. "His work should not be that important."

As Mrs. Kozad continued to rub her hands together, Ruth asked, "Is there more to this story than you are telling me? You seem very upset and afraid. I am wondering if, for example, you might fear that your husband comes home late not because of work, but because he is involved with another woman?" Mrs. Kozad admitted that she did fear her husband was unfaithful, but she had never been able to admit that fear even to herself. She had told herself that her only worry about the late-homecoming was a worry about her husband's health and about his attentiveness to her. Yet when Ruth said the words, Mrs. Kozad realized how much she did fear infidelity. She had, of course, never mentioned her fear of another woman to her husband; but the fear had already caused much distress between them. Nor had her husband ever asked her why she was so afraid.

While Mrs. Kozad told about herself and her sufferings, her voice took on a definite and increasing whine. When this whining had continued for some time, Ruth interrupted to say that the whining was irritating her. "It seems as if you want me to pity you, and it makes me feel you are full of self-pity. I feel uncomfortable and a little angry. If you keep on whining, I will probably get disgusted with you, and want you to leave."

Ruth's observations led the two women to talk about the whine and its effect on other listeners. Mrs. Kozad said she knew she used it often when she talked to her husband, though she had attempted never to ask for sympathy. Perhaps her husband's reaction had resembled Ruth's—discomfort, irritation, disgust. But despite the many times the whine had occurred in their exchanges, Mr. Kozad had never mentioned it, nor had he expressed in words any negative reaction. "Sometimes he did look irritated or guilty, but he never said he was."

As a result of talking with Ruth, Mrs. Kozad felt she had gained some insight into herself. She realized her fear of her own anger, her self-pitying attitudes, and her tendency to block out from herself and her husband certain emotions and thoughts that she thought might disrupt their relationship or reveal her as a shrew. Thanks to hearing about Ruth's reactions to her, she had some hint of what her husband may have been experiencing. By no means were her problems solved by these insights; she had still to accept and deal with what she had learned about herself; but Ruth's attempts to remain "in the room" did prove helpful.

When Harry Kozad came for his interviews with Ruth, the facts taken alone seemed to indicate that he was simply more interested in his work than in his wife. It was true that he often stayed late at work and spent many evenings in civic or business activities. He told Ruth that since he had not completed college, he felt he had to work especially hard in order to succeed. He was doing well in the insurance business and had received more than one advancement. But, he explained, such success required extra work and much attention, even in the evenings. He said he loved his work and enjoyed the hours he spent at it. He told Ruth he belonged to several civic groups and held offices in two of them. Belonging to these groups was, he said, important to his business. These were the facts and they *seemed* to point to the root of the marital problem: too much concern with his work, too little time at home.

Yet, non-verbally Harry Kozad was communicating other aspects of himself. First of all, his posture and facial expressions communicated something other than a hard-working, successful insurance man. When he first met Ruth face-to-face, he looked as if he were cowering in fear. Often during their conversation, he held his hand over his mouth so that sometimes Ruth had difficulty understanding him. He seldom looked into Ruth's eyes. And, although he spoke mostly of his wife's need for counseling, he himself often lowered his head, and his posture seemed to beseech Ruth for assurance and encouragement.

As the conversation continued, Ruth told Mr. Kozad what she was observing in him, and she expressed her own feelings about him. Was he afraid to let her help him? Was he afraid even to communicate with her, even to let her hear what he was saying? Did he fear that what he had to say was really worthless? It took some time for Mr. Kozad to realize and to accept what Ruth was saying. Finally, though, as he and Ruth continued to examine mostly his non-verbal communications, he came to admit that he was afraid he was worthless and had therefore to work hard and to achieve in business and civic groups in order to gain prestige and acceptance. He did love his wife, but he was afraid to tell her that he loved her. He feared any show of weakness before her, any show of needing her. And yet he realized that he desperately needed to hear from her that she loved him and valued him. But he could never ask her how she felt. Since she seemed not to love him, he sought to replace her affection by achievement in business and civic activity. He simply could not tell his wife he needed her assurance and her love. As for muffling his voice, he actually was afraid of being heard, because he was sure his opinions and his inner self were worthless and empty, very far from meriting love and praise.

When he was able to admit that he needed Ruth, Kozad became very open with her and let her see what he considered his weakness and shame. Near the end of the interviews, he told Ruth how much the relationship between the two of them meant to him. Although Ruth was older than he, her acceptance of him, her deep concern, and her honesty in responding to him had shown him that a woman could like him and stay with him even when he had let her see his trembling, his fear, and his inadequacies. Again, Ruth's "staying in the room" did not solve all the problems. But her attempt to remain in the present with Kozad did have recognizable advantages and many good outcomes.

After a few months of separation, the Kozads began living together again. Many difficulties remained; they had to put into practice the results of new insights into themselves and their relationship. But one of the major helps to their succeeding in the relationship was, they told Ruth, their attempt to be aware of their own feelings and to express them openly, no matter how difficult or dangerous that expression seemed. They made some real attempt to remain present to each other. Ruth's "staying in the room" had helped them directly and had been a living model for them in their relationship with each other.

3. The Human Counselor

The Fear of Being Human

Expressing the feelings and thoughts you are experiencing during the interview is a primary way of revealing your humanity to your client. And it is this revelation that, in our view, best facilitates the goals of counseling. But the counselor who does express himself openly and honestly to the client involves himself in risk.

If you decide to be the human counselor in this way, you probably introduce yourself to some hard personal struggles. Expressing feelings and attitudes is not easy. In the most ordinary circumstances, with our closest friends, we usually find it very hard to tell these persons of our affection for them, or to articulate the anger, boredom, or tenderness we might at that moment be feeling for them. All the more so is it difficult to express our inner feelings toward another when that other is a person who has come to us for help and who looks to us for enlightenment and strength.

Fear for Self

Why is it so hard to express our feelings about another to that other? Probably one answer lies in our fear of self-revelation. We are convinced that our inner self, our real self, the center of our personal feelings, attitudes, and responses, is a weak and shameful self, one that would excite ridicule or disgust. Sometimes we are sure that no one else feels as we do, and that our feelings are wrong, warped, or ridiculous. If we reveal this self to others, we may lessen their regard for us. Surely they cannot care for such an odd and weak and pitiful creature as ourselves. So we must remain hidden. Even when we admit to ourselves what our feelings are, we often try very hard to keep others from discovering them.

It would be helpful if such attitudes left us when we became a counselor; but we soon discover that we are indeed still human, still afraid to reveal our inner selves, still expecting to win respect and regard by presenting a false self and by keeping our feelings and responses well-hidden.

Another reason why revealing feelings honestly to another is difficult is because it is uncommon. Sometimes it is considered bad form, bad manners, uncharitable to tell another what is really going on within us as we converse with him. Expression of disturbance or of affection equally are deemed inappropriate in many situations. Better, says the code, to hide your real feelings and to say what you think the other person wants to hear or needs to hear, or what you want him to hear for your benefit. When, then, in a counseling session, you decide to reveal your feelings and thoughts to the other person, you do often act against an unwritten code. Such violation adds to the usual human fear of telling another about your inner self.

But these reasons why we are afraid to express feelings to others fall short of explaining the phenomenon. Best now to rest with the fact, and to go on from there. If you are going to be a human counselor, if developing the human relationship between you and the client is important to you, then during the actual counseling sessions you will be called upon to reveal your current thoughts and feelings to the client; and such self-revelation will probably cost you dearly in fear and embarrassment. The expression will frequently be awkward as well as difficult. To live out this part of the counseling relationship, then, asks of you a willingness to take risks. It asks personal courage and even an abandonment of sorts—you don't know the outcome; you expect the worst; you trust the best will happen.

Fear for the Other Person

For, added to this human fear of expressing inner feeling is your regard for the client. Surely, you think, if I tell him what I am feeling and thinking about him, I will hurt him. I will lower myself in his eyes. I will cease being the tower of strength he needs. He won't trust me anymore. Or, maybe I will embarrass him or hurt him or reduce his self-confidence. Perhaps I will drive him away. Often all these reactions occur when we are about to express affection or fear or disturbance or wonder or any of myriad other emotions to the client. We fear for ourselves, and we fear for him.

And it is probably only through putting yourself in the place of the client and seeing the situation through his eyes that you, as counselor, can see why your expression of feeling, with all its awkwardness and difficulty, is crucial to the development of your relationship and to his growth. From the viewpoint of the client, the counselor's self-expression seems worth the cost in fear, embarrassment, and courage. From the client's viewpoint, it could almost become a rule for you, the human counselor, always to express what seems to you most difficult to express, for that expression will most likely be exactly what the client needs most to hear at that moment in the relationship.

Let us, for the moment, take the client's viewpoint in certain situations where the counselor does express his feelings. One such situation is not uncommon. It is the one where you are preoccupied with some other matter when the client is speaking to you. For instance, just before the person entered your office, you received a letter telling you that a close friend is ill. Shocked and concerned, you cannot help being preoccupied with this news even when the person seeking your help sits down in front of you and begins to talk. From your viewpoint, there are many reasons why you should refrain from mentioning your preoccupation to this person. After all, it is your personal business. You fear that by mentioning a personal difficulty you will lose the "proper distance" between you the helper and the one being helped. Moreover, not being able to dismiss the preoccupation when professional matters demand your attention does seem to be a weakness; and it is difficult for you to tell another, especially a client, of your weaknesses. But above all, you want the client to know you are really interested in him. If you tell him you are preoccupied with another matter, surely you will reduce his trust in you.

Now, for the moment, put yourself in the position of the client. While he is talking of matters important to him, he notices that you are not paying full attention. Perhaps your eyes seem vacant or distant as you look at him; or your comments are perfunctory, not quite to the point. Even your effort to pay attention strikes him as just that—effort. He realizes that somehow he is failing to command your attention. Being human, the client will tend to interpret the situation in the worst light. He will probably think he is the cause of your difficulties. He will tend to judge that you are bored with him, that you find him strange, dull, or crazy. He may feel that you are rejecting him, and with good reason; he may assume that he is telling you the "wrong thing," and that he has therefore bungled things again. In his mind he is to blame for your preoccupation with other matters and for your having to make an effort to listen to him.

Let us assume that despite your fears of doing so, you do tell the client that you are preoccupied with another matter. You tell him you have just received some bad news and you find it hard to focus your attention on any other concern, no matter how important. The admission may come out a bit awkwardly and with an apologetic air. What now does the client probably feel? First of all, relief. You are telling him that he is *not* the cause of your inattention. He is not boring you; he is not saying the wrong thing; he is not leading you to reject him. His relief will often be visible, and some-

times he may even tell you that he is glad "it wasn't me."
Secondly, by telling him of your preoccupation, you are
confiding to him something human and personal about
yourself. Entrusting the client with this piece of your
humanity can increase his belief that you genuinely wish
to enter a real relationship with him. Finding that you,
too, are human can relax him and bring him encouragement. You are telling him that he is not the only one who
lacks perfect self-control.

The Way to Be Human
Expressing Disturbance

As a next example, we can consider the situation in
which your preoccupation does arise from something in
the client. Perhaps some mannerism or some constantly
recurring phrase such as "you know what I mean" dis-
tracts you or gets on your nerves. Or perhaps the person
keeps repeating himself in a way that disturbs you. Even
in these cases it seems better for you to tell him why
you are disturbed. He is probably picking up the signals
of your disturbance and wondering what he is saying
or doing wrong. Usually he thinks the worst. He is sure
that his revelations are disgusting you, and that he is
indeed a shameful human being.

If you do tell him that some *mannerism* disturbs you,
he will probably once more experience relief because now
he knows that your disturbance does not arise from
something terrible in him. A mannerism isn't so bad,
when the cause could have been his shameful, guilty

revelations. Since it is hard for anyone to hear that he isn't perfect, the person may become a little nervous and on edge when he hears that he has a pesky mannerism. But despite this reaction, this person is probably admiring you. If you can tell him honestly about his mannerisms and about your disturbance, he can admire your courage and openness, and he can believe all the more that you are really going to "level with him." You are not just going to tell him everything is beautiful, when he knows everythiɪg is not beautiful. Once more, any awkwardness you may show only increases his belief in your honesty with him.

Expressing Your Weaknesses

Among the hardest things to express to a client are what you consider your weaknesses. When they are actively present during an interview, you may find yourself struggling hard before you can bring yourself to express them. Here blind faith is often required, because at the moment it seems that only embarrassment to you and harm to the client can result from such a revelation. What you consider your weaknesses can include almost anything in you that does not fully measure up to what you think you should be. No matter what others say about it, you are sure that a "fully functioning person" or a "good counselor" should not feel what you are feeling. On the other hand, perhaps you are called upon to express what you think the client will see as a weakness in you. You yourself may not consider it a weakness, but you think the client would call it that. In either case, expression of weaknesses is usually difficult. But it is also most helpful to the client.

Let us say that during a counseling session, you have become involved in the client's world. You sense his needs and his call to you; and you long to help him. You yearn to be able to bring him the brilliant insight, or at least the response that will touch and heal. If only you knew what to say or do; for now is the moment, it seems, when the perfect word would transform this man. But the truth is, you don't know what to say. You don't have an insight into what is really happening in the client. You, too, are bewildered. All your attentiveness, concern, and empathy seem to have resulted only in your sharing the client's confusion. At this moment you feel that you have failed as a counselor. After all, you ought to bring strength and enlightenment, but instead you are lost. You may wonder what the client would think if he knew you could not bring him any insights. Surely he would end his relationship with you. But if at this moment, you decided to be truthful with the client, his response might surprise you. In expressing your weakness, you might say something as plain as, "I really don't know what to say to you. I wish I did." You are, in your own judgment, admitting failure at your task.

What often is the client's response to such an admission? Sometimes he will agree that you are failing him. But more often than not, he will find in your words comfort, encouragement, and relief. After all, he, too, has experienced failure in perhaps many of his tasks and relationships. He has had the fear that unless he accomplishes a given work or meets certain standards, he is not worth anything. Moreover, he has probably experienced great fear of admitting to anyone that he has failed. Perhaps he has spent much time and effort covering up his shortcomings at work or in his responses to people. So here you are telling him by your admission that (1) it is all right to feel inadequate at a job; (2) it is all right to be honest about this failure, both with oneself and with others. The client can find in your admission real encouragement, because, despite your inability to provide a helpful insight, he still values you and considers his relationship with you of great importance. He would be dismayed if, at this moment, you terminated the counseling relationship. He sees, then, that even though you have failed in some part of your task, you are by no means worthless. So, perhaps when he fails at a task, he is not automatically a failure as a person.

He sees, too, that neither you nor he received irreparable harm from your admission of weakness. Your honesty did not destroy him, or you, or the relationship. Perhaps he, too, can someday express to others his real feelings even when these are feelings of inadequacy and failure. Far from condemning you, this person has found in your response a workable model for his own more open and honest responses to others.

During an interview a counselor told his thirty-four-year-old client that he did not know what to say to him. He added, "Unless I can explain or bring insight to you, I feel useless." "Oh God," cried the client, "that's the last thing I want!" Sometime later when the series of interviews was drawing to a close, the client said to the counselor, "Of all the things you have told me, the most helpful have been the things you called your weaknesses. A couple of times you told me you didn't know the answers when you thought you should know them. You told me you had had homosexual feelings. You told me when you were afraid or tired. When you told me things like this, I don't know why, but I always felt a whole lot better. I wanted to let you know about my reaction because I suspect it's hard for you to let somebody else see you aren't perfect."

Revealing Selfishness

Perhaps what you find difficult to express to the client is simply that you are too busy or too tired to see him. For example, just as you were ready to leave your office at the end of the day, a student or a fellow worker comes in and asks to see you immediately. He has a problem, and he wants to talk right now. If you tell him you are tired, you are postponing help for him. Let us say that you tell him honestly that you are tired and perhaps won't be able to listen to him very well. If he can make an appointment for a later time, good; if not, you could spend half an hour with him, but you tell him you are too tired to remain longer.

Or perhaps you are very busy. A person comes as if expecting you to drop everything and bring him immediate help. You tell him that you don't think you can talk to him at all at this time because you are very busy; and you suggest that he see you at some other time. In this situation you are the selfish one, and the one responsible for postponing help. What will the client think of you? Will he think that you are uninterested? Perhaps. He may very well be offended and disappointed in you, and he might not come back even if he says he will. On the other hand, your honesty might amaze him. How often he has wanted to say just that to others who have come to him, or, in a thousand varying circumstances, to people who were bothersome to him. You didn't pretend with him; you didn't display a strength that wasn't there; and at the risk of his displeasure, you didn't lie. He senses, even in this small instance, that here is a person he can believe and trust. And if it is all right for you to say such things to him, a person in distress, then it is all right for him to be honest with others even when it means delaying help. Far from bringing destruction, such honesty, he finds, has some kind of magic for bringing persons together. They sense they can trust each other, for it is their real selves present in the relationship. Often, after all, we want nothing more than that.

The following is an actual incident in which the "I am busy" did have some good effect. Mary, a university student, came in the early afternoon to a counselor whom she had several times consulted at the university counseling center. She said she needed to see him and seemed to expect that she would be ushered immediately into his office. The counselor told her that he was booked for that afternoon and asked her to come back the next day. Upset by this response, Mary made no move to go but instead fired questions at the counselor. "Do you really believe all that crap that you told me? I can't accept it. The whole thing sounds phoney to me." She then challenged something specific from their earlier interviews.

The counselor responded simply: "I do believe what I said to you, and I try to live by it. But if it isn't a truth you want to live by, or one that you experience as true, I wouldn't want you to follow it."

At this Mary fell silent. Once again, the counselor
suggested that she return the next day. Obviously angry,
Mary left the office. She did not return the next day, nor
did the counselor hear anything more from her until two
months later when he and the girl met accidently on
campus.

Mary seemed very pleased to see him, and asked, "Do
you remember that day I wanted to talk to you, and
you said you were busy? Well, I was really mad at you,
but I'm a lot better off now because you didn't see me."
She told him that because she couldn't talk to him that
day, she was forced to face up to her crisis alone. "I
realized I had become dependent on you to tell me how
to live my life. If I didn't consult you on a problem,
I was lost. Well, that time I couldn't consult you." She
faced her problem alone, and came out of the situation
well. Her experience proved that she herself was capable
of dealing with the disturbing elements in her life.

She went on to say how surprised she was that the
counselor had not "dropped everything and listened"
when she had made such a strong plea for help. The
reality of his having other relationships and other ob-
ligations not subject to her control helped her to realize
that she, too, had "reality limits" in her life. "Somehow
I was taught by what you said—that you were too busy.
It had never hit me that you weren't available to me
for all the time I wanted." She remarked, too, on the
few sentences the counselor had spoken to her that day.
In them he had admitted that he might be wrong, and
that what was true for him might not be true for her.
"You admitted that you could fail. And you told me
that I could not take your words as the infallible guide-

lines for my life. When my fury died down, I saw I would have to live my own life. Now I know I can do it. So, thanks."

Sharing Human Nature
Sharing Deficiencies

When a client tells you of what he considers a serious deficiency in himself, you can often help him, not by trying to minimize the failing, but by admitting that you share that deficiency. A case in point is a client's occasional attraction to suicide. Such an attraction often seemed to him a livid proof that he is abnormal. Only "crazy" people have, in his opinion, suicidal tendencies. He may quickly add that he does not desire to shoot himself or in any way actively to end his life—"There are just times when I wish I would slowly dissolve." Hidden in his statement may be the appeal, "Is this a sure sign I am psychotic?"

Although probably most people at some time or other have felt the attraction of suicide, very few ever admit to such a feeling. Perhaps the client has never heard a "normal, ordinary" person admit to a real desire to have his life end. While we easily joke about wanting to commit suicide, we seldom seriously admit to such a desire. The client's conclusion is, "Anyone who wants to die is abnormal." He is probably at the same time tense and afraid in the presence of his crazy feeling.

A major help to him now would be to hear some ordinary person whom he considers normal admit to feeling at times a desire for suicide. You are the person with him at this moment; and you, being human, have probably experienced in some way the feeling he describes. But it may not be easy to tell this person that you have felt as he feels. For, once again, the presumption is that the counselor is indeed normal and that the person seeking help is the weak one. The client comes to the counselor for strength, insight. Surely he does not need to be told that the counselor, the pillar of strength, is as weak as he is.

But if you can tell him that you have shared in his "deficiency," then you do give him an opportunity to relax about his feelings. Maybe they aren't the sure sign of abnormality. Maybe ordinary people do experience them. Perhaps he will see that he has these feelings more often than he should, but he can also see that the feeling of itself is not abnormal. He can, therefore, accept himself better. He can even reduce some of the tense vigilance that has accompanied these feelings. By telling this person that you share his feeling, you have probably relieved him of fears, doubts, and unnecessary self-condemnation. And you have done so without trying to minimize the significance of what he has told you. He still knows you take his feelings seriously. But he also knows that he is not alone in feeling as he does.

Expressing Affection

It is usually difficult for a counselor to express affection to the person coming to him for help. Expressing affection to anyone in itself involves risk. In the counseling situation such expressions are inevitably awkward. You wish you had said it better. You wish your embarrassment had not shown through. You wish your fear of laying yourself open were not so obvious. But here again your awkwardness can be your ally. It helps the client believe you. If your expression of caring and affection comes out awkwardly, the other person has strong proof that it isn't just so many words. It must be true; otherwise you wouldn't endure pain to say it.

And, once again, you have modeled behavior for this person. He, too, finds expressions of affection difficult, and he runs from them. He, too, stumbles in awkwardness and embarrassment if he tries to tell another that he cares. So why bother to pay the price? Better to keep feelings to oneself. But now in the counseling situation, he sees you struggle with your fear, and he hears you express your affection with difficulty and awkwardness. He concludes that it is, therefore, more than all right to tell another of your affection for him, and to stumble and be embarrassed in the telling. If the counselor can be awkward, then surely the client can be allowed awkwardness in expressing affection.

But the cost to the counselor should not be minimized. If you decide to express your affection to the client, you will probably have to struggle with many opposed feelings that warn you not to lay yourself open, not to invite this person's overaffection or his scorn. Also present is the fear that your hearer will simply ignore your awkward expression. But, if you are the human counselor, and if you do experience affection and concern, you may decide in the face of your fears to take the risk; and you will probably find the result well worth the daring.

Here is an example. Jackie, a young woman whose

upbringing and present situation were harrowing, had acted like an automaton throughout the counseling interviews. Each time she came, she droned out her story of tragedy, suffering, and despair. As she recounted situations and events, she showed little feeling beyond a stoic, matter-of-fact, hopeless facial expression and voice tone. Evidently her attempts to deal with the accumulating sorrows in her life had left her finally numb, cold, and impervious to feelings. She seemed unable to find anything positive in her life, and nothing positive appeared in her early counseling interviews.

Jackie's story and her present condition aroused the sincere concern and sympathy of the counselor. He felt warmly affectionate toward her, and often shared her depression. During the early interviews, he told her of his concern and sympathy, and he tried to listen without prejudice to everything she said. As the bleakness continued, he even began to dread the weekly conversations because they were so depressing.

Finally, during one interview he himself was overwhelmed with feelings of bewilderment and helplessness; at the same time he experienced his genuine affection and concern for this unhappy person. For a while he struggled with himself whether or not to do what his human feelings urged him to do. Should he break what he thought were hard and fast rules of counseling? What if other people found out? Finally, despite his fears, he decided to give some expression to his feelings of affection and concern. Embarrassed and awkward, he stood up, walked to Jackie and, without a word, took her hand in his and held it.

There was a pause; then Jackie clutched his hand with

enormous strength, and burst into tears. Continuing to hold his hand, she sobbed and sobbed for nearly ten minutes without speaking. This was the first time during the months of counseling that she had displayed any emotion. From that time on, the counseling took a much more positive and successful direction. Jackie could feel again, and she let herself experience long-repressed emotions of sorrow, despair, anger, revolt, and finally, affection and hope. The counselor's simple gesture, which had cost him so much in fear and embarrassment, had to his own surprise broken the baneful spell.

Expressing Fear and Anger

What about expressing to the client your negative reactions to him? If you feel anger or fear, for example, should you tell him so? From the counselor's point of view, many factors argue against such expressions. You could discourage the person, add to his depression, make him dislike you, turn him away. But, from the client's point of view, the situation appears in a different light.

Perhaps, for example, you are frightened for this person. You are afraid he will get into trouble. If you tell him you are afraid for him, you fear he will think you are saying, "You're really sick." But what he actually may hear is this: "I care about you; I am concerned enough to be frightened for you." The expression of negative feeling helps him believe in you and develops the healing relationship between you.

Perhaps you experience anger during an interview. This person is forever telling the same childhood experiences. He is avoiding you and hiding his real feelings.

You have told him all this several times, but he doesn't seem to hear you. Finally, as he continues the game, you become angry, and you show him that you are angry. He will probably feel hurt and become angry, too. But in the exchange of negative blasts, he discovers that neither you nor he has been destroyed. Showing anger does not necessarily crush people and break friendships. The client may somehow grasp that "Maybe I, too, could let out my anger to someone else. Maybe I could cleanly tell somebody off, get rid of the anger, and I wouldn't destroy that person or make him hate me." It is possible that this person has never before experienced a clean blast of anger from anyone. He discovers that, like the genuine affection he experiences, genuine anger need not be absorbing, consuming, and destructive. And, once again, your honesty with him reveals more of your real self to him, and deepens the human relationship between you.

Lack of Expression

Perhaps it will be helpful to consider what might happen if you decide not to express your feelings to the person seeking help. For example, let us say that a young man has told you that he fears he is homosexual. Saying this to you has cost him a lot, and he considers his revelation shocking. Perhaps you are disturbed by what he says, but you do not want him to think of himself as shameful and disgusting because of his tendencies. You yourself have perhaps experienced such feelings in the past, and you know from your counseling that many persons have homosexual feelings at some time or other. But because your feelings are mixed and because you do not want him to think his feelings are really shocking, you decide to say nothing. But what does the person read in your silence? Being human, he focuses on the worst possible interpretation of your lack of response. He concludes that you are rightfully condemning him.

It seems better in such a situation for you to tell the person that what he says does disturb you, but, because you have talked to so many who have homosexual tendencies, and because you have had them yourself, what he says does not overwhelm you. If you admit to the disturbance you do feel, and add the other thoughts his revelation brings, then at least he knows you are not feeling the stronger emotions of disgust and horror. You are not condemning him. Any sincere response to his very difficult revelation seems better than none at all.

A similar situation occurs when the person tells you that he often feels dislike and even hatred for his parents. Since we are all supposed to love our parents, he considers himself somehow unnatural, the worst person that ever lived. If after such a revelation, you remain silent, he may read in your silence, "You are bad, ungrateful, inhuman." It seems better to tell this person, "I think I understand your feeling of dislike and even hatred for your parents. Sometimes I've had feelings like that myself. In fact, all the time I seem to have a combination of positive and negative emotions for my parents. And many people I've talked to have felt dislike for their parents and have condemned themselves for feeling like that. We all think our relationship with our parents should be loving and wonderful, but often it isn't. Maybe the child-parent relationship is the hardest one of all." Some such words let the client know that he is not condemned.

4. The Bond Between Persons

The Need for Friendship

Two problems that often plague a counselor are these: Should I allow myself to become emotionally involved with the person who comes to me for help? And, what if he becomes too dependent on me? In this chapter we will discuss ways that remaining human with the client can give some assistance with these problems of involvement and dependency.

First, involvement: Should I let a bond of affection develop between me and the client? Should I make some emotional commitment to this person? Should I allow myself to care for him so much that, whatever happens to him, I am emotionally affected? Should I allow such a bond to develop between us that I can bring personal pain and hurt to the client, and he can bring personal pain and hurt to me? Should the client and I really become friends? Should I, in other words, "get involved"?

These questions are serious, and the responses can be frightening. If you do become what we have been calling the "human counselor," if you do permit a real human relationship of concern and warmth to develop as the chief contribution of your counseling, then the questions about emotional involvement with the client will arise because the human relationship we speak of consists, for the most part, of mutual emotions. Here we will explore the counselor's fear of involvement, the real risks it entails, and the rewards which this involvement can bring to the client.

The Fear of Involvement

If you choose not to become involved with the person coming to you for help, your basic reason for refusal is probably fear. If you do choose to become involved, you have probably faced some fears and are taking risks in your choice. Whatever way you choose, it is best to admit these basic fears. What are some of them?

First of all, there is the fear of being responsible for something harmful or tragic in another person. If you were to remain humanly uninvolved, you could still bring help to this person. You could listen, analyze, interpret in a helping way. But if you were really to care for the client, if you were to feel genuine affection for him, you might speak to him in a way that will open him up to his deeper sadness and terrifying yearnings. You might ask a question that prompts this person to examine and to expose disrupting, shattering, life-changing feelings. And you would be, in part, responsible. You might feel yourself responsible for this person's taking drugs, giving in to homosexual tendencies, or attempting suicide. Better, says fear, to remain aloof—attentive and concerned, but personally uninvolved. Better to offer the educated analysis rather than the personal question.

Again, if you become personally involved with the client, he may respond to your personal questions with personal questions of his own. He may ask you about yourself, not as a "counselor" but as this human being. You may well fear your reaction. Could you endure such questioning? Would you be honest and genuine? Would your response injure the client?

You may also fear the extremes of the client's response to your personal commitment to him. The client might resent you. He might take personal revenge on you or on those you love. He might become dependent upon you, or fall in love with you. On your part, if you allow personal emotions in yourself, you might develop parental attachment to the client or you might fall in love with him.

And underlying these fears is the desire to protect yourself from being hurt. If you really care about this person, you give him the power to hurt you. His responses can bring you pain, embarrassment, and sorrow. It will make a difference to you emotionally if he resents you, does not respond to you, or decides not to return for further interviews. Even when the natural end of the counseling interviews arrives, it will be hard for you to say goodbye to someone you really care about.

Another fear about involvement with the client can be simply a fear of surrendering too much time to him. If you show personal concern, will he begin to make unrealistic demands on you? Will he pester you with phone calls and beg for more frequent visits? And if he does make such demands on your time, will you be able, when

the situation calls for it, to say no to him? Will you be
able to refuse his demands at the risk of his rejecting
you? Will you be able to meet his possible objection that,
"You say you are my friend, but you don't have time for
me when I need it."

Finally, you may experience the fear that you will not
be able to be both friend and counselor to this person.
"Counselor" seems one role, "friend" another. How can
you effectively be both? Will not "friend" ruin "counselor"? Perhaps the most helpful way to meet this fear
is to question the seemingly great difference between
friend and counselor. Perhaps if a counselor is not a
friend, he is not a counselor. Perhaps the best way of
counseling is to be friends with the client and to respond
to him then spontaneously, as friend to friend. But the
fears of such an approach are indeed large.

For you do take real risks if you become involved with
the client. Many of the things you fear will probably
happen. You may be hurt; the client may react in a way
you do not want; he may make unrealistic demands on
you. But unless the relationship between you is alive
enough to make these real possibilities, then it is probably not a genuinely helpful relationship. It may be a
helpful analysis, but it is not the sort of human relationship which we consider central to counseling. This latter
relationship draws two persons together emotionally. The
therapy lies in the reality of this bond. This sort of human counseling incurs serious risks. What should you do
if what you fear does occur? There are no answers beyond saying, live out these occurrences humanly. If the
client falls in love with you, deal openly with this love
and with your response to it. If the client hurts you, deal

openly with this event in your relationship. In becoming a human counselor, you take personal risks. No one can say where your involvement will lead you.

The Rewards of Involvement

Will the counselor injure the client by responding to him humanly and personally? This question has no universal answer. Injury is always possible, and personal involvement surely risks it. Perhaps the further question is more helpful: Can the counselor's involvement bring rewards to the client that make the risk of injury worth taking? To examine this question it seems best to take the client's point of view.

The client is someone so confused and upset that he has chosen to seek help from another person. As we have said before, although the client often asks help on a specific problem, he is normally bringing to the counseling interview much deeper problems about his own person and his relationship with others. He is bewildered about his feelings and attitudes. Perhaps he doesn't yet know what most of them are. He is frightened by what he does know of himself. Whether consciously or not, he is asking for help in exploring the unknown and repellent regions of his dark self. Consciously or not, he is asking the counselor to care enough to come along on the fearful exploration. Only someone really interested enough to hear and to offer acceptance and encouragement, even in the face of the "terrible" in the self, can qualify. The client is looking for a sympathetic, interested human being who, responding humanly, can be a companion on the inward journey. A cold demeanor, an uninvolved ap-

proach, well-controlled and hidden emotions are probably not the qualities the client, knowingly or not, seeks
in the counselor. The client wants someone who will care
enough about him to be affected by what he tells him. He
needs someone who, humanly moved by his plight, will be
with him with human warmth, acceptance, and concern.

The client needs to feel that another human person is
accepting him as a person, and precisely as *this* person
with all his disturbing qualities. A "professional" attitude
of approval may fall short of what the client seeks. He
needs a person whom he can trust so that, drawing comfort from this trust, he can get out of himself all the
things that bother him. It is the comfort of a trustworthy,
concerned companion that he seems to need in order to
display, even to himself, the shameful or fearful things
demanding expression. Most helpful to him here would
seem to be, not analysis, but genuine affection and genuine
interest—both emotions of involvement.

Often the person seeking help fears that he among his
acquaintances and daily associates is the only one who
experiences certain shameful or disruptive feelings. Or, if
he suspects others may feel them too, he is often sure that
he is the only one among his associates who experiences
these feelings to such an alarming degree. These feelings,
then, make him label himself "abnormal," "perverted," or
"insane." While he attempts to hide these feelings, he
is at the same time considering himself unworthy of the
respect and concern of others. Yet the feelings he experiences, even the degree to which he experiences them,
are often very common; many people experience them.
But the point is that few people ever reveal to another that they have these feelings. Not many people

talk at all about their inner responses and tendencies, especially about the ones they are ashamed or afraid of. Perhaps the client has seldom or never heard another "ordinary person" speak of his own homosexual tendencies, or his dislike of a loved one, or of his great loneliness beneath an attractive and lively exterior.

What does such a client, then, consciously or not, look for in a counselor? Probably for another human being who can express to him personal feelings like his own. Such expressions depend on the counselor's genuine involvement.

The client may also look to the counselor for another kind of human expression which few people have the courage to make. He needs to know how his personality affects others. Is he disgusting and unattractive to others? Why does he have such difficulty making or keeping friends? Is there something about him that frightens people off?

Most people, if they find the client disturbing, will not tell him so. They will often remain pleasant but aloof while the client does not understand the reason for their aloofness. If, for instance, without realizing it, he is making heavy demands on a friend's time, that friend will probably *not* say outright, "You are making heavy demands on my time." There will be evasions covered up by pleasantry or even over-effusiveness in giving untrue excuses. In a counselor, then, a person might well seek someone who is not afraid to say outright what his responses are, negative or positive. On the counselor's side, of course, such expressions are risky because, coming from him as a person, they may invite genuine personal responses from the client. These responses can evoke a whole range of emotions, all of them some form of human involvement.

In this same vein of wanting to know how others really respond to him, the client may also seek in a counselor someone honest enough to ask questions that might be difficult to answer. Politeness and role-playing are baffling smoke screens the client has encountered often enough. What he wants is a brave person, interested enough and honest enough to ask what should be asked if the client is to be honest with himself and with others. Here again, the counselor is asked to take personal risk, for his questions may evoke similar ones from the other person. Or they may lead the client into dangerous areas of the personality where he may find threatening aspects of himself that could lead him to personal injury or injury of others.

If we consider again that the client's difficulties are usually to a large extent interpersonal, then again an "involved" person may be the sort of counselor he is seeking. He needs to know that he is capable of exciting another's concern, interest, and even affection. He needs to know that he as a person can excite these responses in another human person. A counselor, responding humanly to the client, is to that extent emotionally committed. If the client discovers that he can relate personally to this one other human being, he can find basic insights into how he can relate properly to others. If he feels he has made a friend during his counseling sessions, then he has taken the first huge step toward working out his whole interpersonal problem. Once the client has been open with one person who has responded to him as a person, it is not easy to turn back. He has experienced the bond, and this experience has illuminated and released powerful natural tendencies which are not easily made prisoner again. But for the client to experience such a bond, he needs a counselor who has allowed his own emotions to come into play. Unless mutual human feeling and expression are alive in the relationship, then the relationship has not been the sort to model future relationships or to fully release the client's emotional tendencies toward closeness and openness with others. Here more than anywhere, the answer to the client's problems lies, not in professional knowledge or analysis, but in the person of the counselor he talks to. He seeks a counselor who, as a human being, gets involved.

The Threat to Friendship
The Problem of Dependency

What do you do when you realize that the client is becoming dependent on you? He seems unable to make a decision without consulting you. He must seek your approval for practically all his actions. He must constantly phone you or write you or see you. This problem of dependency can arise especially if the counselor is inexperienced. Although anxious to be human and concerned, he is not fully aware of the responses of the client or indeed of his own responses. He may not realize what is happening until the problem by its very grossness strikes him. Yet the problem of dependency can arise in any counseling relationship, even when the counselor is a professional psychologist with years of experience.

It can arise almost everywhere. A teacher, accessible

to students between classes, at lunchtime, and during office hours, can become an easy target for a dependent young person. Although officially seeing the counselor-teacher only one period a week, a student-counselee can manage to run into the teacher often, he can just drop by the classroom, and in this way he needlessly consumes much time and energy, to his own detriment and to that of the teacher. Sometimes a wise and understanding housewife, whose home is open to grateful young people or to neighbors seeking help, finds herself bombarded with lengthy telephone calls or with prolonged and unseasonable visits. The lawyer whose human concern has allowed him to listen to his client and to touch upon the central conflicts behind legal problems can suddenly find himself bombarded by a series of unreal legal "needs" of the client. There always seems an excuse for a call or a consultation. For whatever reason, the problem of dependency can loom large, especially if the counselor has allowed himself to become humanly involved with the client.

How can you deal with this problem? First of all, it is necessary that you be alert to signs of growing dependency in the person seeking help. The signs are often obvious: the person asks your approval constantly and refuses to act without first consulting you. He must call you any time of day or night if something unexpected arises, or if he is simply afraid. The problems he brings up, both in and out of the counseling sessions, seem ruses to gain an extra talk with you or to prolong a session. If you are counseling him in informal circumstances, without a clear time limit to the sessions, he may stay for an extra hour or two as he repeats his story and questions you on unreal or minor difficulties.

He may, without directly asking your advice or approval, find it necessary to describe in detail what he thinks is right or what he did or plans to do. He is asking you to pronounce "right" or "wrong" on what he seems so sure about and yet must lay out before you in such detail. He may accuse you of not responding to him, of not calling him, or answering his letters, or arranging extra interviews. Surely you do not "care." Sometimes the main sign of the client's growing dependency is your own feelings of being drained or consumed by him. Sometimes the tip-off is the client's seeming immunity to ordinary social sensitivities. He never knows when it is time to go.

The Safeguards
Against Dependency

Know Yourself

What is happening in you, the counselor, is extremely important. It is possible for you to cause or increase the client's dependence on you because of needs in yourself. You may be dependent on him because you need love and comfort not found in your daily living. You may need all the reinforcement he can give of your power to influence people and to win affection because, in yourself, you are so unsure of your worth and attractiveness. You may need a proof of your "success" as counselor. Although all of these needs and feelings are often present in the counselor, their excessive presence can silently invite the client to a dependency not helpful to him. Here it is important that the counselor know and accept his own feelings and honestly come to terms with the difficulties he himself faces in the counseling relationship. Discussing the problems with the client may prove very helpful in alleviating the mutual dependency or in terminating the counseling with least hurt to the client.

In addition to recognizing any dependency in yourself, it is important to be aware of all your feelings when signs of the other person's dependency appear. And it is important to express these feelings to him, despite the difficulties involved. Yet, becoming aware of the feelings may in itself pose problems because you may fear that your suspected feelings of boredom, anger, or "being had" tell you that you are not what you want to be— that is, you are not the concerned and empathetic counselor. Fear of failing to care may cause you not only to overlook your own real feelings, but it may also cause you to increase your signs of concern. You may begin, half unconsciously, to display insincere emotions in order to convince the client, and yourself, of your interest and involvement.

Express Yourself

It is better simply to admit your fears and discomfort, your resentment and feelings of being consumed. Expressing such feelings to the client poses new problems since often when a person is dependent, the counselor can have the sense that one more "withdrawal" will be too much for the person who sorely needs affection. But, if the relationship is to develop honestly, and if the client is to grow personally, it seems better to tell him that you fear he is growing dependent, that you yourself feel "used," drained, and uncomfortable. You may decide with him on limits to your conversations, to the number of visits or calls. While you are doing these things, you will probably need much courage and trust, for it can appear that you are destroying the relationship and the other person—and yourself as counselor.

If the person does not seem to hear you but instead continues his dependency practices, it is sometimes advisable to ask that a third person be introduced to help decide if the relationship should be ended. Sometimes continued and excessive demands, in the face of the counselor's honestly expressed feelings, are signs of deep-seated problems for which this person should have further help beyond ordinary counseling. Yet, even when this is the case, it is highly probable that your sincere concern for this person and your honesty with him have brought him new insight and new confidence.

Often, however, when you tell the person of your fears of his growing dependency, and when you and he discuss new limitations on, for example, the number of conversations, the client will respond in ways most helpful to his own growth. He will probably experience some pain and resentment. At first, he may have suspicions about your concern. But he may also discover again the depth of your concern because you have dared to be so honest with him. Now, if you tell him you like him, he will believe you.

He may realize that he does not want to become dependent; and, when you tell him your fears, he may for the first time be able to recognize in himself attitudes he does not want to develop. Although pained, he may also be grateful especially when he finds new powers in

himself for decision-making, for establishing relationships, and for developing his relationship with you. He
will soon discover that the limits you set free both of you
to have a more mature and satisfying relationship. Consuming another is no longer the only way to keep a
"friend."

Your honesty may help bring order into his chaotic life.
Perhaps his inordinate leaning on you is only part of his
general disarray. He may be unable to "hear" others and
to gauge relationships and situations with balance. Not
understanding others, he sees no way of making contact
other than by bludgeoning people with his dependency
on them. His responses and demands are chaotic and
unreasonable. Since few people will be honest with him
for fear of hurting him or themselves, his "friends" soon
mysteriously terminate the relationship. Now, you come
along and, feeling what others feel, you *tell* this person
that you like him, but that you feel he is consuming you,
choking you, and not hearing you. Together you discuss
the limits your relationship must have if it is to exist at
all. You regulate conversation times, phone calls, notes,
and "chance" encounters. As you tell him of your other
friends, other interests, and other commitments, he can
painfully realize that his needs cannot rule your world,
or, in fact, *the* world. You do not exist just for him, and
yet you do care about him. This new sort of relationship
can be very instructive. As he runs up against the hard
reality you show him, he may begin to see other hard
realities he has overlooked. It is important to remember
that the "reality" you have shown him includes you and
your real concern for him. He can see then that limitations need not destroy a relationship; they can, in fact,

help. As order and balance emerge in your contacts and conversations with him, he may begin to experience and to bring about new order and balance in other areas of his life. This result is, at least, one to be hoped for as you face the pain of ending dependency.

Examples

We will now give some examples; the first will deal with the problem of involvement; the others describe situations of dependency.

Larry, an undergraduate English major at a state university, was greatly disturbed by his own strong homosexual tendencies. He did not want to be homosexual; he was dating a girl he liked very much, and he hoped to marry and have a family. He was handsome, imaginative, and sensitive. He was definitely attracted to other men, but he had not engaged in any overt homosexual activities. Although he was a very good writer, he avoided writing fiction or poetry for fear he would reveal his despised tendencies. Finally, in his junior year, he brought his problem to a university counselor, Mr. Gilbert, a young man just out of graduate school.

The counseling interviews lasted, off and on, for the last two years of Larry's university courses. During that time the boy was able to face and accept his tendencies and to allow his love for his girl and his desire for marriage to develop. Encouraged by his conversations with Mr. Gilbert, he told his girl about his homosexual tendencies, and together they worked out the problems that arose during their dating time. Not long after Larry's graduation, they were married. About a year later, after Larry had taken a job and his son was born, he stopped to see Mr. Gilbert when he happened to be near the university on a business trip.

During the interview Larry revealed that he had recently contemplated suicide. Harassed by financial problems and sure he was failing his wife and child, he had taken a piece of rubber tubing to the basement and had intended to inhale toxic gas. But as he was attaching the tubing, he had been overwhelmed with fear and regret, and he had abandoned the plan. Now he was full of guilt about his intentions. Finally, as he finished his story, Larry burst into tears. The sobbing was so hard that he could not walk. He got down on his knees and crawled across the two feet of rug between him and Mr. Gilbert. He put his head in the counselor's lap and sobbed, "I love you, I love you."

What about Mr. Gilbert in all this? At the beginning of the counseling sessions, he had feared allowing himself to feel affection for Larry, much less to express it because of the boy's admitted homosexual tendencies. Gilbert found in himself some homosexual inclinations which he feared could be aroused by the relationship. How could he help the boy if he allowed him to know that his counselor loved him? But Gilbert did come to have some real affection for the boy. He knew there were some homosexual overtones in his own affection, but that these were not dominant or destructive. Once he explained briefly to the boy how he felt, and Larry seemed to accept this expression with simplicity and appreciation. He encouraged Larry in his plans for marriage, and watched happily as the boy began freely expressing himself in creative writing.

Only when Larry returned after his first year of marriage did Mr. Gilbert experience how strong his own love was for the young man. At the moment Larry, weeping and crawling toward him, had cried, "I love you," Gilbert felt himself undergo a profound change. He felt his own spontaneous love well up. What he experienced seemed to transcend questions about "what kind of" love. Knowing the risk he took, he let himself feel his own emotion and accept Larry's love. No one had ever touched him so deeply before. He felt that this young man had released his own pent-up ability to love. Instead of repelling the sobbing man, or attempting to play down the explicit expression of love, Gilbert accepted it and said, "Larry, I love you, too."

The very deep love that had always been implicit in the relationship was now out in the open. Larry could finally express it, and Gilbert could finally accept both Larry's love and his own feelings. They both discovered that when the feared expression had come out, it was not so frightening. It was accepted by both and could be dealt with in the concrete. Both accepted their love with its varying homosexual overtones. They were able to discuss it and come to terms with its problems. Again, to their surprise, the homosexual overtones receded; the two men experienced a free and healthy love without the feared tendency to sexual expression. Larry felt triumphant and reassured; he could openly love another man without being drawn into what he considered abnormality. Gilbert was able to feel and give love in a way new to him and most welcome. Yet neither felt drawn to any expression of affection other than a gentle embrace. When they parted that day, both were changed men, and much happier.

*   *   *

Miss Jones was a popular high school biology teacher who was available during several study periods and after school for students who requested her help either as teacher or personal counselor. Several times she had experienced the difficulty of telling students that the conversation was growing too long. She set no limits to the talks, and sometimes she had to manufacture excuses to end the interviews.

Marie, a high school senior, especially engaged Miss Jones's attention and sympathy. Marie's real parents were divorced. The mother, who received custody of Marie, remarried twice. Becoming an alcoholic, she finally abandoned the girl who was then taken into custody by a cousin of the mother. This cousin was a convinced devotee of a small religion which scorned advances in science as the work of devils. When Marie took Miss Jones's class, she experienced a great many confusions and fears. These difficulties formed the basis for the first conversations between Marie and Miss Jones. Soon, however, Marie's deep-seated troubles about human relationships came to the fore. The girl distrusted everyone, and said that she expected every so-called friendship to end in betrayal, or at least in accidental disaster.

Miss Jones became deeply concerned about Marie. Sensing that the girl needed someone who could love her and could prove trustworthy, she encouraged Marie to visit her office, to take noon-hour walks with her, and to contact her whenever the girl felt frightened or when she had some good news to share. Soon Marie's visits became more frequent and seemingly endless. She seemed at last to have found a trustworthy adult friend, and all her thoughts now seemed to revolve around Miss Jones.

While the absorbing relationship grew, Miss Jones, with the best of intentions, continued to reassure Marie of her affection, and continued to pretend interest and enthusiasm that she did not genuinely feel. Thinking that the girl needed love, she tried to force herself to provide that love. She tried to supply as best she could under the circumstances the motherly care she knew Marie had never experienced. Yet much of this care was forced, and Miss Jones began to experience weariness and even aversion toward the client. Despite her own discomfort and tension, she continued to allow Marie to set the time and length of the interviews.

By the time Marie had graduated and begun college work in another city, the relationship had become one of extreme dependence. Letters came to Miss Jones two and three times a week. Marie made special trips to spend part of a weekend with her idol. Miss Jones's tensions increased as she became more and more perplexed about how to handle the absorbing but debilitating love she had inspired. She feared that showing any lessening of affection would plunge Marie back into her former attitudes of extreme distrust. Miss Jones did not want to add another betrayal to Marie's list.

But finally, after one of Marie's visits, Miss Jones decided to write a candid letter in which she honestly expressed her own feelings to Marie. In it she reaffirmed her affection but also told her that she found herself consumed by Marie's many communications. She said she thought Marie was becoming dependent in a way that was proving injurious to the girl's growth and to their own friendship. She asked that their relationship be continued on a more mature footing, that it become, not a quasi-mother-daughter affair, but a genuine relationship between two adults. Miss Jones rewrote the letter several times, fearing that Marie might even contemplate suicide if she were to interpret the letter as another betrayal. Finally, still unsure of the wisdom of her action, she mailed the letter.

Nearly two weeks elapsed before Marie answered. When she did respond, it was with the most mature and balanced communication Miss Jones had yet received from her. The girl had obviously suffered but had also understood Miss Jones's words and intentions. She agreed to write much less often and suggested that she visit only at Miss Jones's invitation. This letter set the tone for all her subsequent communications.

Meanwhile, Miss Jones had undergone many struggles with her own emotions, and had finally admitted to herself that she had forced attention and concern in ways she had not really felt. She admitted her weariness and discomfort and even her occasional dislike for Marie. Her own communications assumed a more genuine and simple tone; they no longer attempted to salvage Marie by great shows of affection.

Several months elapsed before Marie visited Miss Jones. When she did at last appear, the girl exhibited far less dependence. She had begun developing other relationships, and spoke with Miss Jones in a much freer and less grasping way. As for Miss Jones, she was both surprised and happy to discover that once she had admitted her negative and guilt-laden real feelings, she had somehow freed herself to experience genuine warmth toward the girl. She felt sincerely glad to see Marie, and found herself experiencing sincere affection for her. From then on, the relationship continued in a much more relaxed way, and in a way that led to the growth of both client and counselor.

*   *   *

A middle-aged nun, Sister Ellen, experienced many changes in herself when she returned to school for a master's degree after she had been nursing for over twenty years. During her studies she had encountered new people and ideas, and, thanks to the friendship of several people at the school, she began to experience feelings and attitudes she had not been aware of before. When the changes became baffling, she consulted a trusted clergyman who encouraged her to accept her feelings, and to explore more deeply into her personality. As the one-hour weekly interviews continued, Sister Ellen grew frightened of the attitude changes in herself, and she became increasingly dependent on the encouragement and acceptance of the counselor.

As this dependence became more apparent, Rev. Smith discussed it with his client, and, after some anger and disagreement, Sister Ellen was able to agree that she was placing too much of her life in his hands. But the problem was complicated: Sister Ellen was discovering that she had been living for many years according to what she thought others would think of her. She had been guided in many decisions and attitudes by what she thought rules, superiors, nuns, and patients expected her to be. Outside standards had been her touchstone of self-evaluation. So deep had been this dependence that, in recognizing it, she fell back, not on her own resources, but on the judgment of the trusted counselor. As the path of independence opened for her, she fled from it by finding dependence elsewhere.

A critical moment for both dependency relationships came when Sister Ellen recognized and admitted to herself and the counselor that she did not want to return to the former position she had held in the hospital operated by her religious community. She wanted instead to undertake a kind of public health nursing in a large city. Such a position was open to her, but accepting it would mean not living in one of the community convents. It also meant leaving unoccupied the important position she had held in the hospital. Finding a replacement would be difficult. Other nuns had taken positions similarly independent; but Sister Ellen felt that her personal needs made her decision especially difficult. It was no longer a question of asking permission; it was, rather, a matter of announcing that she was going to begin the new work after her studies were completed that summer. Pretending to ask permission was a deception she did not want to practice. She feared that her superior and the community council would rebuke her for her decision, and would ask her to choose between taking the position or remaining in the religious community.

In fact, the superior and council had previously acted in a most liberal way; but Sister Ellen, from the center of her personal fears and doubts, really believed that her membership in the religious community was at stake. She was terrified at the thought of being asked to leave the community because she liked the life of a nun, she liked her community, and feared having to begin a life on her own as a middle-aged, single woman. She had grown overweight and was, she thought, past the age of attracting a husband. Living alone was a horrifying prospect. She felt old age was not far away, and she had no security in family or money to meet it unless she remained with her community.

Yet, to be true to herself, she felt she must take the risk of losing her community membership. Several times she asked her counselor if he thought she should take the risk. He refused to express either approval or disapproval, but instead he told Sister Ellen that he wished the decision to be entirely her own. He spoke again of the dependency he feared from her.

Finally Sister Ellen wrote the letter. But, before mailing it, she asked the counselor to read it. Assuring him she asked neither approval nor disapproval, she told him she simply wanted him to know what she had written. But once again, he refused to take on any of the responsibility of her decision. He refused even to read the letter. The actual mailing of the letter cost Sister Ellen a high price in emotional upheaval. Without sharing the responsibility with anyone, she had placed her former life in jeopardy. By her own decision and action, she had risked causing herself to become what she had always feared and despised—a single, middle-aged, unattractive, lonely career woman.

But the action alone of mailing the letter seemed to set in motion new feelings and attitudes. During the week that followed, she began to experience new strength and endurance along with her continuing fears and doubts. Her superior responded favorably to Sister Ellen's decision. There was no need to consider ending her membership in the community. On the contrary, the superior commended her and encouraged her. By the time the superior's letter arrived, Sister Ellen was already more in charge of herself. She did not contact the counselor until the ordinary weekly interview occurred. At that time she told him calmly of the letter, and expressed her gratitude to him for refusing to take responsibility for her and as well for making her aware of how dependent she had grown, both on the opinions of her sisters and on his judgment.

The therapy interviews continued for another month. Then, by mutual agreement and despite fears still in Sister Ellen, the formal counseling was ended. Several months later, Sister Ellen completed her studies and assumed her new position. Although she still experienced many difficulties, she wrote to the counselor later that "mailing that letter by myself was, I think, the turning-point. Thank you for being cruel."

*   *   *

Bruce, twenty-three, and Shirley, twenty-nine, were both graduate students in counseling psychology at a university. Both were single and had become friendly acquaintances by being in several classes together. In one laboratory class they were teamed as facilitators for an ongoing encounter group of high school students. They enjoyed working together and met each week at the graduate student union to discuss the group. Thanks partly to the atmosphere of the counseling psychology department, they felt free to be truthful and open with each other. Over their coffee one day they both expressed their affection for each other and felt happy at the rich relationship they had.

After this conversation, Shirley began to call Bruce to ask advice, and several times she arranged to meet him for what became counseling sessions, with Shirley as client, Bruce as counselor. Bruce, glad to help his friend, was patient with the phone calls, attentive during the "coffee" counseling sessions, and flattered by Shirley's attention and trust. Before the semester was over, however, Shirley was bombarding Bruce with calls and demands. She accused him of not living up to the love he had expressed for her. Bewildered, Bruce repeated that he did indeed love her but not in the way she apparently thought he did. He was not "in love" with her, did not want to marry her. He told her what she already knew— that he was very serious with a girl in his home city, and that he was hoping to marry that girl.

Still Shirley refused to hear Bruce. The calls continued; at their weekly conference sessions she often made demands on him, although just as often their conversations were deep and interesting. Soon she began writing letters to him. Matters were complicated by the necessity of their being together in their classes.

Finally Bruce told Shirley as clearly and honestly as he could that he did love her, that he was not *in* love with her, that what happened to her did matter very much to him, that he was in love with and wanted to marry another woman, that he did not wish to hurt Shirley, that he thought she was dependent on him, with her demands. He then asked that she cease writing and calling him. For a while Shirley obeyed, but within ten days she was again sending notes and making "short, necessary" calls. At last Bruce refused to open the notes; when a call came from Shirley, as soon as he recognized her voice, he hung up. But still the calls came.

Finally, wracked by her accusations and demands, Bruce suggested that together they consult a third person, a faculty counselor who knew both of them. By this time Bruce felt guilty and afraid that he had indeed led Shirley into false hopes and expectations, and that he was at least in part responsible for her present suffering. The viewpoint of a third person could help them decide whether or not to continue their relationship. Shirley agreed to the consultation.

During the interview with the faculty counselor, Bruce explained his attitudes during the relationship and repeated in some detail what he had often told Shirley about his feeling of friendship toward her, his love for another woman, his plans to marry, and so on. Shirley reacted bitterly and accused Bruce of being, she said, "sick and dependent, even though he keeps implying that I am the sick one." After questioning Shirley for some time, the counselor told her that he thought she was refusing to "hear" Bruce. "Right now while Bruce was talking, you seemed not to understand him. I felt that when you responded to him, you were responding to some imaginary person who wasn't here at all." Shirley remained silent during the rest of the interview. At the end the counselor said he would be glad to see both of them again, but separately. When he finished speaking, Shirley turned to Bruce and accused him of pre-arranging the interview and of telling the counselor what to say. "You don't want to come here with me!"

After that consultation, Bruce refused to communicate with Shirley beyond the usual greetings if they met in the classroom. At the close of the school year, Bruce returned to his home city to be married. When he and his wife returned the next fall to the university, Shirley had prematurely terminated her graduate work and was living in another city. Bruce received a brief note from her saying that she planned to marry soon. Bruce continued to feel guilty and concerned; but he felt that he had acted as best he could in carrying through a most difficult "counselor-client" relationship.

* * *

Paul was a young social worker who, on a volunteer basis, counseled boys at a large Eastern reform school. One sixteen-year-old, Randy, responded very well to Paul and was eager for friendship and help. The boy was warm-hearted, sociable, and intelligent. He had a rather long police record which reflected his upbringing in slum dwellings and foster homes.

The counseling went very well. Randy wanted to learn, and, with Paul's encouragement, his grades began to improve, and his total outlook seemed brighter and more forward-looking. Paul himself was elated with the progress of his client, and he went eagerly to their weekly interviews. The boy's approval and affection brought encouragement and reassurance to the counselor. It was not until several months had passed that Paul began to realize how dependent Randy had grown. Earlier Paul had helped Randy work out a schedule for study. Randy was proud of his fidelity to the schedule, and several times he told Paul how well it was working. Then one day he asked Paul if it would be all right to use the whole one o'clock period for English rather than math since exams were coming up. The boy's request for permission to make a trivial schedule adjustment forced Paul to recognize how dependent the client had become. Paul realized that he himself, glad for approval and for the progress of his client, had encouraged this dependence. He himself had become dependent on the boy for encouragement in his own work.

Fearing to hurt the boy's progress, Paul took his problems to a friend who did professional counseling. After listening to the story, the friend said to Paul, "I agree that Randy has become too dependent on you. But the problem is yours. You have come to me for a solution. I have no solution. Go back and work out the relationship in your own way."

The friend's refusal made Paul realize that he himself was showing a dependency very much like Randy's. When the problem became really difficult, he had immediately sought out an "authority" who would know the magic formula for dissolving the trouble. Now Paul realized there were no magic formulas; the solution to the problem lay with Randy and himself. They would have to "work it out."

When he saw the boy the following week, he told him his fears about the dependency. They talked and talked that day; from that time on, Paul tried in every way to help Randy assume responsibility for his own life. The boy responded. He seemed to understand the problem and he wanted to be on his own. At first he made small decisions about his study time and about the choice of a course. He triumphantly related each incident to Paul. Then little by little he was making more decisions on his own and was initiating activities without asking either before or after the event for Paul's approval.

The counseling seemed headed for a happy ending. Paul was leaving to take a job in another state, and Randy was becoming independent. Then one day the boy shocked his counselor. He said, "This is goodbye, Paul. You've been great. I won't see you again before you leave because tonight I'm going to escape." And that night Randy did escape. Paul did not hear from him again.

Paul was left in confusion. Had his attempts at "freeing Randy" led to the boy's injury? Was Randy misusing independence? Was the counseling a failure? Should he have insisted on professional help? Yet the boy *was* more mature, more responsible, or was he? Were all Paul's attempts to free his client for personal responsibility just leading up to an event which seemed at least dangerous to the growth Randy was exhibiting? Paul experienced feelings of guilt and failure; yet he could not say for sure that the boy's escape was wrong nor that the counseling should have taken another direction.

5. Counseling in Other Professions

This book is filled with examples because examples alone will illustrate the kind of truths that can be only vaguely touched upon by theoretical considerations. Yet there is also a necessary limit placed upon the number of examples that can be included in any book. This imposes a burden on the reader. He must translate the message contained in the theory. He alone knows his own personality and circumstances well enough to make the practical application necessary for his counseling. Finally, he will have to rely upon the experience of success and failure to discover the best way for him to become a human counselor.

This present chapter is an attempt further to aid the reader in bringing theory into practice. The few illustrations presented here do not begin to solve all the problems implicit in the experience of counselors. Our hope is that the examples given will present an approach to experience that will profit the counselor who would like to bring more of himself into his counseling.

The Lawyer

As a professional, a lawyer may consider it sufficient that in the interviews with his client he gain the legally pertinent information about the client's status, requests, and needs. If that client could fill out blanks in a detailed questionnaire, he would satisfy the purpose of the interview. It is possible that the client as a human person is barely present to the lawyer. Perhaps the client will leave feeling that the lawyer has not really understood what he wanted, although all legalities have been cared for.

On the other hand, many lawyers want to perceive and respond to their clients, not as mere legal entities, but as human beings filled with emotions and attitudes which influence the legal proceedings, and which have an important human bearing. The client as human person in relation to the lawyer as human person becomes important in the interview. The legal interview, while focusing necessarily on pertinent information, becomes a human conversation, and the lawyer, in many instances, becomes a real counselor.

One example to consider here is the person who comes to a lawyer in order to make out a will. Such "estates planning" requires that the client confront the fact of his own death. In doing so, the client may have strong negative emotions: he does not want his experiences to end; he fears for his dependents; he is unsure of an afterlife. In addition, death is, so to speak, socially taboo, a topic usually avoided, a fact to be ignored as much as possible. Talking directly about one's own death, even to a lawyer, may prove difficult and unsettling. The client also faces the fact that his property as well as other persons in his life will remain after he is dead. This prospect can bring discomfort; or, more usually, it can give the client a feeling of immortality since something of himself will continue beyond his death. He may also have various emotions about his spouse or his children or others who depend on him. He may fear that his wife will remarry or that his children will not have a college education. Perhaps another emotion is present: he may have decided to make out a will at this time because someone close to him has just died. When he comes to the lawyer, he may be grief-stricken.

It is quite possible that the wills client does have some of these difficult emotions. It is also possible that he is not able to identify them or to confront and accept them. He may not realize the emotional influences on him. Before he will be able to identify and accept his unpleasant but important feelings, he may need understanding and acceptance from a person he can trust. What the client needs, then, is not just a master of law, but an interested, open, and caring human person.

If the lawyer is willing to enter into the human dimension of the interviews, he can bring immense help to the client by providing an atmosphere in which fears, doubts, worries, sorrows have a chance to show themselves without being condemned. The lawyer can try to understand the client's world, to reflect it back to him, to remain aware of and respond to verbal and non-verbal communications, and in all these ways to relate to him in a warm, accepting human way. In such an atmosphere of freedom and acceptance, the client may be able to identify, clarify, accept, and work with the often unwelcome emotions influencing him. The lawyer, by "remaining in the room" as a responsive and understanding human being, can help this person accept himself and confront realities which are unpleasant but which under the circumstances must be faced.

If the lawyer does relate humanly to his wills client, he may find himself called to express what he feels even though he risks offending. For instance, a client may continue to insist on a trust fund that would make remarriage difficult for his wife. Or he may continue to want money allotted in ways so specific that the guardians of his children would be unrealistically restricted in their care for those children. If the lawyer is feeling uncomfortable and disturbed with the client's views, it seems well for him to express his feelings. He could tell the client that he is sorry about the client's views and that he himself feels that the client, by making these dispositions, would bring hurt where he wants to bring help. By expressing his own feelings in this way, the lawyer does not impose his views on the client or claim that he, the lawyer, has the right viewpoint. But this expression might well help the client realize what his own fears are and how they might bring injury to others.

The wills client is only one of a multitude of persons who come, under circumstances of strain or difficulty, to the lawyer. With these others as with the man making a will, the lawyer can, if he wishes, become a human counselor willing to "stay in the room" with another human being. By doing so he can help free these clients to face and accept themselves in the face of the often emotional situations which have brought them in the first place to seek legal help.

The Nurse

In this section we will consider the nurse as counselor in
her relationship with the ordinary medical-surgical
patient and with the patient diagnosed as "mildly depressed." In speaking of the nurse, we hope that what we
say will apply also to the licensed practical nurse, the
nurse-aide, the orderly, the volunteer worker, the physical
therapist, the technician, and to anyone else working
with patients in hospitals.

Everything we have said before about the counselor
applies, we think, to the nurse. As we have said of the
counselor generally, it is important for the nurse to be
aware of herself, her own emotions and reactions; that
she trust herself, her hunches and her feelings; that she
respect the patient as a human being who thinks and feels
even when he is sick or overwrought; and that she interact with him honestly.

Temptation not to be herself with the patient can
come in many forms. A common temptation is to look and
act "like a nurse"—that is, to play the professional role.
Encouraged by her uniform, by the institutional atmosphere and by the heavy workload, she may cover her own
personality with a cultivated tone of voice, and a brusque,
cold but technically efficient manner. Perhaps inwardly
afraid for her image and afraid to reveal lack of knowledge or judgment, she will maintain a closed and well-
guarded exterior.

Another way for her to close off her person is by
treating patients like unconscious objects. She never en-

ters a human relationship with them. They are to be kept clean, fed, and medicated. They may be dressed, moved from bed to chair, walked after surgery, wheeled to labs and therapy rooms. They can be fully classified, examined, diagnosed, and administered to, all without any human contact having taken place. In outpatient sections or emergency rooms, for example, a nurse could receive a patient without greeting, attend immediately to the problem at hand, and never let the patient feel that he as this certain person has entered the nurse's field of awareness. Yet at this moment, another human's acceptance of him, his pain, and his fears is what the patient needs.

A nurse can cut herself off from patients by distrust. Especially if she is unsure of herself, she may suspect that the patient may deceive her; and so she protects herself by maintaining an attitude of suspicion. She may expect bungling and weakness from the patient; she may fear that he may make her look foolish or may challenge her authority if she trusts him. He might, in other words, penetrate her defenses. When a nurse maintains such an attitude toward a patient, she makes any counseling very difficult. If she were to use counseling techniques, these would be gravely weakened because her own defenses keep her real person from the relationship. Her distrust, which she herself may not fully acknowledge, would prevent the development of an accepting relationship. She would be incapable of taking risks.

Understanding Illness

The nurse as counselor needs to understand what illness can mean to a person hospitalized for ordinary medical-surgical reasons. Becoming ill and living for a while in a hospital can for many people be the first chance they get in many years to be themselves. They know they are forced to waste time. It's all right to relax and to take one's time. No one will condemn the sick man if he doesn't produce. There is time for thinking and reassessing. Relieved of normal pressures, he may find himself thinking new and perhaps disruptive thoughts.

It is all right for the hospitalized man to let his "weaker" emotions arise and to give expression to what appears shameful in him in ordinary life. He is permitted to be sad, to have self-pity, to express his loneliness and depression. He can get angry because he has such a good covering excuse. He can be warmly grateful to those who help him; he can express affection because, after all, much is permitted to the unfortunate sick person. He can allow himself to face feelings of hostility because he has a good excuse to ask for "no visitors." He lives in a socially acceptable atmosphere for the feelings he may have feared and kept hidden. He may feel himself a free man.

It is here where understanding and acceptance become very important for the nurse as counselor. The sick person is a human being perhaps wrapped for a long time in a well-defended business or social role. Now in the presence of the nursing staff, he is being more of himself. What he needs often is for someone to be with

him and to accept what "comes out." He will give verbal
and non-verbal cues of his emotions: he may say outright
what he is thinking and feeling; he may ask for things
without apparent reason; he may have a distracted look
or make remarks that invite attention; or he may show
seemingly unwarranted concern or joy over something.
In whatever way he communicates his need, the nurse
who is interested in counseling can pick up the cues and
respond to them as honestly as she can. She can tell the
patient what she thinks she perceives in him. She can
respond to his outright statements about his feelings:
"I'm glad to hear you expressing these things. If you
want to talk some more, I'd be glad to listen because
I'm interested." She can by her attention and concern
give him the opportunity to explore his feelings. She can
attempt to understand and to let the patient know that it
is all right to allow these feelings to appear. If she has
such an attitude and expresses it, the patient can tell her
the truth—for instance, that he *likes* being in the hospital,
that he dislikes visitors from home or office, that he hates
his work or his falsity at work, that he wants to "get
away from it all"; or, on the other hand, that he feels
unwanted or simply "used."

When he is talking, the patient is probably not asking
the nurse to do anything. Talking itself is a great release
for him. The nurse's interested and human presence is
what he needs most. Here the nurse will have to trust
that she is "doing something." But honesty remains
extremely important. As the patient is communicating,
the nurse may want to contradict him. If so, she can tell
him of her impulse. If she feels sympathy or distress or
joy, telling the patient of these feelings is important. If

she owns her emotions and impulses as her own and does not force them on the patient, her honesty will, as we have said many times, simply deepen the therapeutic relationship between them.

Sometimes because her time with the patient is limited and his hospital stay relatively short, the nurse feels that she can't do any effective counseling. She may be right in given instances. But sometimes only brief talks over a short period of time are enough for the patient to get the things he needs most. He needs release from his immediate and often self-imposed responsibilities; an opportunity to let his real feelings arise; a human being who has genuine interest and concern, who will let him talk and explore, and who, despite the consequences, will let him know honestly how she feels about him and about all he is saying. Thanks to these factors, he is able to release something natural and healthy in himself. One taste of such freedom and truthfulness may be all he needs to begin seeking more satisfactory ways of living his daily life. Many nurses know from long experience that former patients remember exact words of a helpful conversation. "I never forgot what you said. It really meant a lot to me." Or, "It changed my life."

Counseling Depressed Persons

Sometimes a nurse is called upon to help a person hospitalized briefly because of "mild depression." While this term can cover a variety of things, it often means that a person has broken with his usual world by means of an "illness." This illness could be an experience of overwhelming fatigue which has no adequate physical cause.

At a certain point his whole person reacted to his life in such a way that he finds it impossible to do much more than sleep. He may not talk to others. He cannot work. He may experience profound fears and live in half-fantasy. Often it is a great relief for him to come to the hospital because to him hospital means privacy, rest, attention, and care, and above all, escape from the situations and persons which he found impossible to cope with any longer.

We will mention here only that what we have said generally in this book applies even to the nurse's necessarily sporadic counseling of the mildly depressed person. Forming a somewhat satisfactory human relationship is very important for this person. His role-playing, often with those closest to him, has become too much for him. He doesn't want to be false anymore. Sometimes he does not see his situation that clearly; he does not realize why he has to withdraw from people. He simply fears people, fears the old relationships, and deals with them by withdrawing from as much human contact as possible.

The nurse will do little good by trying to cheer up this person; nor will it help to tell him there is nothing wrong with him and to please "snap out of it." Such talk merely reassures the patient that still one more person does not understand. What helps is being human with the patient. The nurse can tell him she is interested, that she understands something of what he must feel, that she knows the process of becoming depressed took a long time and that the process of coming out of it will take a long time, too. It is important that the nurse really understand how slow the reorganization process can be and what strong inner obstacles the patient experiences even in the presence of what seems so simple. The nurse can help by sharing with the patient her experiences of being depressed. Since she offers no quick cures or oversimplified solutions to his distress, the patient can feel that the nurse does understand, is interested in him, and is with him in his quite real suffering. She is giving him a chance to be his perhaps repulsive, irresponsible, evil self—his "new self"—the one that has repudiated his former ways; and in the presence of this ambiguous self, the nurse seems unafraid and accepting. More than that, she can talk humanly with this "self," react to it, respond, share experiences with it. She can tell this real self her desire to "cheer him up," her frustration at having no solutions, her desire that he would try to work or eat or talk. She can show him interest, anger, impatience, acceptance— all the emotions she experiences when she is with him. The patient's relationship with the nurse who is herself with him can be the first step in his forming again some kind of satisfactory relationship with other people. He may, trusting this person of the nurse, respond to her suggestions, accept the limits she places on their conversations, and he may begin to have again some experience of tender, warm, and responsive feelings.

Especially with the depressed person, the nurse may have to deal with the problems of involvement and dependency. But, as we have said over and over, dealing with them openly, trusting herself and her own responses despite the emotional cost to herself and to the patient will in the end prove the most beneficial.

The Social Worker

The social worker, in his daily round of activities, often becomes the counselor. In his contacts with persons on welfare and even in his paper work involving classification and assignments, he often has the option of assuming a façade or of being himself in a human relationship with others. In the following remarks about the social worker as counselor, we will center on certain difficulties which, though common to most counselors, are usually strongly present for the social worker.

First of all, the social worker has ample opportunity to see himself as "helper" and the client as "helpless." The welfare client is in trouble and comes to ask financial aid so that he will be able to provide necessities for himself and for those close to him. The temptation is to see this person as inept, bungling, and not fully human. He is not to be treated as a human person. The social worker may suspect that the client is at fault for his condition and that he should, for his own good, be treated with a cold, stern, and corrective attitude. He is not given a chance to emerge as this person with these problems in these peculiar circumstances. When the client meets with such an attitude from the social worker, he will probably react accordingly. He will let himself be sullen and dependent. He may lose even more of his self-respect. He may himself turn suspicious and belligerent. Although his need for food and housing may be met, his contact with the social worker will have left him feeling less human and less capable of interacting satisfactorily with others. The social worker may succeed as financial helper but fail as counselor because he has failed to enter into a human relationship with the client.

Another way the social worker can fail as counselor is by closing out the client by a screen of expectations. With the best of intentions, the social worker may immediately classify the client on the basis of clothing, hairstyle, color, sex, nationality, home location, or age. The worker may think he knows "what to expect" and "how to treat" such a person. Surely, he thinks, there is a helpful way to meet the needs of "this sort of person." The client, then, once more does not have a chance to emerge as this individual with these problems in these circumstances. For example, if he looks young and disheveled, he "must" have certain feelings, thoughts, and reactions. If the social worker is expecting these, he may blind himself to the human person really there, and he may invite the client to react according to his unfair expectations.

The social worker may also close himself off from the client by imposing standards on this person. The worker may think, for example, that "these people don't know how to take care of themselves." They do not keep their rooms or apartments clean. They do not raise their children right. They have all the wrong kinds of recreation. The social worker, without attempting to enter the real world of the client, may attempt to remake him to his own standards and style of life. Such attempts can very easily dehumanize the client and make any satisfactory human relationship between worker and client very difficult. Considering the client as something of a child, the social worker may emphasize housekeeping and family care methods without first trying to understand the client's way of evaluating his own life-style. When the worker shows so little interest in his views, the client may well feel misunderstood, pushed around, and talked down to as if he were a child. He may resent suggestions which, if he thought the social worker were willing to treat him as an adult person, he would accept as helpful.

A social worker's attempt to impose standards on the client may extend even to attitudes about work and self-support. If he does not accept the client as an independent and valuable human being, the worker may tend not to hear how the client judges the working world, money, advancement, and government. Or if he does hear, he may hear only in order to condemn. For example, a young divorced mother may seek welfare help so that she can go to college. Although she is able to get a job and support herself and her child or children, she makes the value judgment that receiving welfare for a while will provide the opportunity she needs for personal growth and social effectiveness. An artist or a poet may seek financial support from welfare so that he will not have to give up creative activity in order to support himself. He views his personal creative growth and productivity as worthy of receiving welfare support as long as there is no other state provision for subsidizing his work. Many such seekers of welfare find understanding from social workers who prize the client's judgment of his own life-style. But other such seekers may meet with thinly veiled disapproval even when their requests for financial aid are met. The social worker interviewing them may not be willing to enter their world; he may

close himself off from the client and remain simply an
aloof instrument of the state. Such an attitude will usually
alienate the client and leave him feeling treated as less
than a human person. He may feel judged as irresponsible, as lazy and even as dishonest.

We have dealt almost exclusively here with negative
aspects of counseling for the social worker in contact
with the client. On the positive side, everything we have
said in this book about developing the human relationship between counselor and client applies strongly to the
social worker. His clients are in financial need; seeking
help from another person may be a humiliating experience for them. When they approach the social worker,
they may feel shame and disgust with themselves. In
such circumstances, the social worker's acceptance of this
person as a person and his willingness to relate humanly
to him may bring greatly needed psychological relief and
encouragement. Very often when the client seeks financial
aid, he does so because of grave problems in his family.
His marriage may have reached crisis proportions or his
children may be ill or he himself may be disabled or
simply unable to find employment. Sometimes he himself
is unable to cope successfully with his society. The personal reasons that bring him to the social worker often
seek recognition and understanding. Because he experiences grave personal problems, he will often welcome
and respond to the personal concern and acceptance of the
social worker even though he would not have asked for
more than financial help. The social worker becomes an
understanding and respectful human being, and his response helps the client face and explore his own problems often with renewed hope. In other words, the social

worker is in a prime position to become the human counselor to persons who gravely need to enter into an accepting human relationship. Since the world of the social worker and the world of the client may be very different, the place where they are able to meet and communicate is the area of shared human feelings. Both are people; allowing themselves to be human, to respond honestly, and to be open to the other is the only way that helpful communication can take place. The only alternative is a clash of world-views with resultant injury to the humans involved.

6. The Counselor in the Group

The Same Person before Everyone

More and more frequently persons involved in counseling find themselves invited to participate in various forms of group work. They may be requested as facilitators for "basic encounter" groups. They may begin using group approaches to their teaching. They may be asked to lead open discussion on a human level among persons in a business or in a profession. They may find that a discussion group which they have moderated wishes to experience a more personal interchange among the participants. They may become "facilitators" at a family gathering or a gathering of young people at the home of interested adults. If they are in the nursing profession, they may be asked to form encounter groups among patients or hospital staff members. If they are in the legal profession, they may be asked to lead groups for other lawyers or for law students who want to learn how to relate humanly to clients.

You, as counselor, may yourself originate groups as a way of counseling. Sometimes you may have too many people coming to you and not enough time for individual conversations; so you suggest forming a group. Or you may form groups because you think that the counseling achieved in the group situation seems speedier and more effective than in individual counseling. In your opinion several persons help one another by discovering that they share the same fears, doubts, shames, and aspirations. What one counselor might overlook in a person is noticed and expressed by a group member who becomes a real counselor to that other member. You yourself as counselor are more open to helpful criticism, even to attack, if you are insincere with yourself or with others. For these and many other reasons you may choose to be a counselor by being a facilitator of a group.

If you do become a group facilitator, you may experience new fears as well as new excitement; and you may feel in a new way a sense of inadequacy. If you do join the group, then about the only sensible advice for you is, "Trust yourself and be yourself."

Creating an Atmosphere

When you enter a group as facilitator, your main question will probably be, "How can I help these people?" As you look into the faces of these many and varied persons, the question may be phrased with bewilderment: "How can I help *all* these people? How can I develop a helpful human relationship with each of these? How can I work through with each person his problems, his explorations of his inner self, his struggles to be himself, his groping attempts to make satisfying contact with others?"

You cannot do all the things you do in an individual counseling session; nor, for the successful issue of the group, do you need to do all these things. Persons interacting in a group will help one another, and the group will develop in a way different from the interplay of individual counseling.

"How can I help these people?" In our view, you as facilitator will be most helpful when you are trying to be yourself and when you are expressing as honestly as you can your real feelings and responses in the group. Our belief is simple: if you express feelings, others will. If you try to become yourself in the group, then others, too, will try to become themselves. And when this occurs, then group "goals" are, in our view, achieved: you, as facilitator, have helped to create and maintain a climate in which each person in the group can discover and explore his feelings, in which he can express to others what he has always wanted to express. You, as facilitator, by expressing your own feelings and by trying to be yourself, have provided encouragement as well as a model and a climate in which a person can discover himself and can form more real and deeper relationships with others.

If being yourself and expressing your feelings are your main contributions as facilitator, then your attitude will set a tone for the group procedures. You will not need to rely on rules of attendance, of manipulation, of control, of directing the group. You may grant much freedom to yourself and to the other participants. Each person, including yourself, may come and go as he wishes. No one needs to say or do anything in the group. No one will be required to contribute to the group. As for the topics brought up or the procedure to be followed, these will remain subject to the wishes of the group, not simply to yours. Your contribution will be, as we have said, not to direct and control, but to be present as honestly as you can. Such an attitude shifts responsibility from you to the other persons in the group. No one is required to do anything. No one has sure guidelines to follow and lean upon. No one can depend on you to show the way and bring solutions. It remains the choice of each participant to involve himself in the group in any way he wishes. You, as facilitator, will find that you must trust others very much, trust yourself and your own responses, accept the risk of failure, and accept criticism from those who demand that you exhibit conventional leadership qualities. But your leadership lies mainly in your being yourself, and so, by example and encouragement as well as by creating a climate of freedom, you can assist others to be themselves.

Threats to the Atmosphere

If you do decide to contribute to the group mainly by being yourself, there will be certain demands you will have to face and deal with.

One demand which often occurs early in the group is "Be a real leader"—that is, give guidelines and exercise directive and corrective control on the group. Persons may demand this leadership of you because of their own confusion and fears about exposing themselves to the new experience of the encounter group. Although for some reason, perhaps unclear to them, they want to be part of the group, they fear being imposed upon or duped. They fear that by some form of trickery they will be betrayed into exposing themselves to their own shame and future regret. If they could hear directives from the leader and experience him as firmly in control, they would feel some security from danger. If, therefore, you refuse to assume that role, you may have to deal with objections, pleadings, and the demand for an explanation. At this moment expressing your own viewpoint and attitudes may prove difficult; but your responses will set the tone for the entire group. The responsibility for the group will rest, not on you alone, but on each member.

Later in the group sessions, you may find the demand for traditional leadership repeated. "This group is too big to let everyone talk." Or, "This room is too small"; or, "Let's go outside under the trees where it's so beautiful." The burden is placed on you, the facilitator, to make the decisions and change the situation. But your response can shift the responsibility back to the group. "Does the group want to break into smaller groups?" Or, "My feeling is that I want to hear what everybody has to say." Or, "Going outdoors bothers me, but what do the other group members want to do?"

If you are this free with the group, you may find that certain members will try to control you or others by threats. The ultimate threat is usually, "I will leave the group." You must simply be prepared to say, "Okay," and allow that person to leave the group. Sometimes a member will attempt to restrict you and the group by saying something like, "I came to this group because I didn't think it was going to be a cry session or end up in a lot of hugging and that crap." A simple response can help remove that restriction: "I am not here to prompt emotions, but if they come, they are welcome. I wouldn't like to think that we would place limitations on what we can feel and express."

Sometimes in a group you may meet the demand, "Be my counselor." Someone turns to you and starts to tell you his story as if he wants you to analyze it and give answers. A person may subtly invite you to enter a one-to-one counseling session that could consume all the group time and prevent any further group interaction. Here again, you can meet this response honestly only by expressing your attitude toward what the person is asking of you.

The Socially Unacceptable Thing

Stepping beyond the Amenities

If your main way of helping the persons in the group is by expressing your own feelings, by trying to be as much yourself as possible, then you will probably have to say and do several things that are socially unacceptable. But, by doing so, you give the group a model of what it is to express feeling and to be yourself even when this means hurting others or exposing yourself to hurt. Such a model can bring great freedom and encouragement to group members struggling to be themselves, but fearing the social consequences.

Let us say, for example, you notice that some one person is emerging as the dominator of the group. He talks much of the time and exhibits power and authority. Some in the group may fear and respect him; others may be glad he relieves them of the need to speak for themselves. But quite a few, and you among them, will probably be disturbed by the domination. Several will wish to "shut that guy up," but will be unable to say anything. If you are feeling disturbed, the best thing to do is to say so: "It seems to me you are trying to dominate this group. I don't want to be dominated by you. I wish you wouldn't talk so much. Also, I'm bored by what you are saying. I think you are getting us off the track." You have not done the socially acceptable thing. You have risked hurting the person, and you have risked incurring his anger and dislike as well as anger and dislike among shocked group members. But you will have expressed your own real feelings despite your fears. You have undoubtedly expressed what several persons were feeling. When everyone sees that neither you nor the person you addressed have been destroyed by your having expressed your feelings openly, they will take courage to do likewise.

Sometimes everyone in the group will be interested in or bothered by some characteristic of a member, but because mentioning their preoccupation would be impolite, they will refrain from saying anything. But if you are experiencing such feelings, you may want to express them despite your social fears. For example, in one group of fifteen persons, there was a blind man. During several sessions no one mentioned his blindness to him, despite the fact that everyone was fascinated by it and by the way he was able to carry on his life almost as if he were able to see. Finally, in one session he said something about his going to a movie. His statement bothered everybody: how could this man enjoy a movie? The facilitator, experiencing this wonder, said simply, "You just now said 'When I went to this movie'—I feel very uncomfortable about bringing this up, but why would you go to a movie since you are blind?" The other members of the group became very uncomfortable when the facilitator failed to go along with them in politely ignoring the handicap.

But the response of the blind man surprised everyone. He was pleased and relieved that the facilitator had mentioned his blindness. "I really want to talk about my blindness, but almost nobody gives me a chance to." He explained that he lived in two blind worlds—one physical, the other psychological. "This last one is really hard. When people are with me, they act as if I weren't blind. They never mention my handicap and speak as if I were as sighted as they. But it is acting—I *am* blind, and I am restricted, and you can't help being conscious of these things at least once in a while when you're with me. The truth is, if people would mention my blindness, I would have a chance to talk about the things that are important to me. I have many accomplishments I would like to talk about. I'd like to tell what I can do despite my blindness, and I'd like to tell what it's like to live in a physically blind world. I have a lot I want to share with others, but nobody will let me share these things. They are afraid of hurting me, and so they help to shut me up in another blind world where they block certain of their own reactions from me and where they do not permit me to express mine. This isn't always true, I know; but it does irritate me because it happens so often. I want to thank you for bringing it up and letting me get these things off my chest."

You may find yourself expressing quite a few other socially unacceptable things if you are trying to be yourself and respond honestly in the group. It may be up to you to tell the clown he is overdoing it now. Nobody ever tells him that outright. In one group, for example, the facilitator, with much fear, told a man that his jokes seemed to be a smoke screen to keep the group from looking into themselves. "And another thing that bothers me," the facilitator said, "is that you laugh at your own jokes—in fact, you lead the laughter like a cheer." Since the facilitator and the "clown" were friends, the confrontation was even more difficult. But the "clown," after some initial embarrassment and self-defense, calmed down in the group, reduced the distracting jokes, and later attempted to examine the "smoke screen" he was throwing up in front of himself. Nor did the friendship between the men suffer.

Touching the Person

Sometimes what you will say will be more positive. Nobody tells the attractive woman she is attractive; everyone thinks the woman knows she is attractive and receives compliments from many people. The fact is usually that nobody tells her she is attractive. Yet, you, as facilitator, may wish to tell her she is attractive. If you do, you risk getting yourself condemned, and you risk offending others who are less attractive than the woman you compliment.

Sometimes you may wonder about a person who seems always light, cheerful, and entertaining. If he has continued this very attractive, pleasant manner during an hour or two of the group sessions, you can usually assume that the way he is in the group is the way he is with others. And the group reaction to his entertaining disposition is probably similar to the reactions most people have to him most of the time. They like him, feel better with him around, envy his lighthearted manner, and encourage him in his behavior. You may wonder if his actions really do reflect his feelings. You may say to him, "You always seem to be so cheerful, and you are always entertaining others, but I wonder do you yourself ever need cheering up?" You risk being wrong; you may cause him discomfort, and take away the group's entertainer. But you may really have given this person a chance to explore and voice other emotions he has concealed from himself and from others.

For example, in one group a young businessman, Mack, had been a lighthearted and very entertaining member of the group for nearly a week. Not only was his conversation interesting and fun, but at the evening gatherings for beer and relaxation, he danced and sang, and did both very well. The facilitator, however, was wondering more and more if this part of Mack were the only part, or if there was hidden in him something darker and perhaps painful. Finally in a group session, the facilitator expressed his feelings to Mack, and asked him if he himself ever felt sad or needed cheering up. Mack answered with a joke, and the group went on to other topics. But on the following day, Mack himself, growing serious, mentioned to the group what the facilitator had asked the day before. "I'd like to talk about that now," he said. And he proceeded to tell the group his own story, a tragic one. Although his lightheartedness was often real, it was also what he thought others wanted from him. He feared relating to others without the guise of entertainer. As he told of the sorrow that was in him, tears came to his eyes. He had never told anyone of this dark part of himself, and merely talking about it brought him relief. After that session he experienced feelings he had shut off from himself and others for several years. The group members helped him, but he found turmoil in attempting to accept all of himself, and to give all of himself expression. A year later he came to see the facilitator, and told him that the remark, "Do you yourself ever need cheering up?" had changed his life. "I even have different friends now. I avoid some people and some places where I would start being just the old entertainer. It still hurts, but it's *right*."

Saying the socially unacceptable thing does not always, even in the group situation, have such a happy ending. The facilitator risks incurring the anger and even the hatred of the person he addresses. He may set off a barrage of defense from both the person he has spoken to and from other group members. Since he is only expressing his own feelings and reactions to the person, he will not be wrong in the sense of falsely judging the person, but he may discover he is reacting to something not really in the person. Or his question, "Are you always cheerful?", may meet with the sincere response, "Yes." The implication of his question was wrong. But at least he will have been honest and will have modeled for others what it is to express oneself sincerely. Even when the response he receives is negative, neither he nor the group members have been destroyed. Being oneself, even when it brings discomfort and anger, need not be destructive; the risk is not too great and the benefits, no matter how it comes out, are of no small worth.

Sometimes the group reactions to the facilitator's socially unacceptable statements are mixed. For example, in a group of twenty-two persons, the facilitator noticed that a girl who had spoken very little was choked up with emotion. Now, it is the more acceptable thing socially to pretend that you do not notice if someone is crying or showing strong emotion. The presumption is that the person is embarrassed enough without others adding emphasis by comments. But in this group situation the facilitator did turn to the girl and say, "You seem on the verge of tears."

Before the girl could answer, an older man in the group shouted at the facilitator, "That's cruel! All you want is to get a display of emotion at this poor kid's expense. You're just a junior counselor trying to show off."

The facilitator turned to the man and said, "I'm not a bit interested in your opinion." Then, facing the girl, he asked, "Did you feel I was trying to provoke your tears?"

She answered, "Oh no, I was glad you said something. I wanted to talk about it." But because of the interruption, she had lost the emotion and could not recapture it.

An Example

Doug and Andrew were invited to co-facilitate a three-day encounter group for thirty nuns involved in teaching and inner city social work. The two facilitators decided to sit opposite each other so that what one overlooked, the other might notice. The group began smoothly enough, with the nuns trying to concentrate on personal expression and interchange, and to avoid centering on their work problems.

On the second morning one pleasant and gracious young woman, Lisa, calmly mentioned some difficulties which several of the nuns, including herself, had experienced with a certain administrator in one of the large city convents. Lisa wondered about how to "change such situations because they really drained people." Others agreed about the difficulties, and an older nun gave a long explanation about why the administrator caused such troubles. She then told Lisa what she considered the best and only way to deal with the situation: "Keep out of her way and act on your own." Another nun contradicted this one, and soon several were offering solutions to the problem.

Then one nun said, "Let's not get off on the topic of administrators and superiors and how to change the structures of convents. We'll end up spending all our precious time figuring out a new government system instead of getting at our own feelings." Many agreed, and the conversation took another direction. Doug, the facilitator who could not see Lisa, joined in the new topic and agreed that "tearing down structures" was not what he wanted to talk about that day.

Meanwhile, Andrew, the facilitator facing Lisa, noticed that the young woman looked bewildered and sad, and that she was no longer interested in the conversation. Her face became flushed, and she seemed close to tears, although she was obviously trying to hide her emotion. After watching her for a little while longer, Andrew interrupted the ongoing conversation, directed his attention to Lisa, and said, "I think we may have been unfair to you a few minutes ago when you brought up that administrator problem. I don't think you wanted to talk government at all. I am wondering if there is something very personal and perhaps very sad that you were trying to tell us."

At this, the whole group turned to Lisa. She was embarrassed, and at first tried to smile in her usual gracious way. Then suddenly she looked at Andrew with a kind of pleading in her eyes. "Yes, you're right. I wanted to say a lot more. I don't know what I wanted to say—except that I guess I've been through hell, and I'm still in it. It's awful!" Tears came to her eyes, and for a few moments she was not able to talk. Then, in a simple voice tone she had not previously used in the group, she told a brief tale of her fear, bottled-up anger, personal hurt, and feelings of despair and rebellion. The other nuns, surprised and moved by the story, responded to her with understanding and compassion. By the close of the session, Lisa seemed changed. Two nuns in particular told her they had seen her in a new way, and felt very close to her. Such contact seemed to bring great relief to the young woman.

During the rest of the sessions, Lisa was much more full of life, much stronger, and able to speak openly and sincerely to the other nuns. Tears continued to come to her eyes, but she told Doug and Andrew during a coffee break that "I've lost a huge burden; I feel like a new woman." Her administrator difficulties were not solved, but thanks to Andrew's embarrassing intervention, she had let her inner self be seen; and her sisters had not rejected her. She said she no longer wanted to be the perfectly gracious Lisa, known for her self-control and unfailing calm. The tumultuous and complex Lisa had shown through and had not destroyed anyone. She thanked Andrew for turning the gaze of the whole group on her show of weakness. And Doug apologized for ignoring and misinterpreting her.

The Dimensions of Risk

It is seldom easy to tell someone your real feelings about him, especially if that feeling is affection. To say, "I like you" or "I feel very close to you" is risky because the response of the other person could bring you hurt, embarrassment, or shame. If you show this tender part of yourself, you risk its being rejected or ignored. If it is accepted, embarrassment and regret can follow. What, then, about a facilitator's expressing affection in a group? First of all, he takes the common risks that accompany any expression of love or concern. Secondly, he risks making a public show of his hurt at rejection or his shame at being ignored or misunderstood by the person he addresses. In addition, by expressing affection to a member of the group, he does the socially unacceptable thing. For he very well may hurt other members of the group who might think he doesn't like them. Why does he show favoritism? Why does this person draw the affection of the facilitator instead of that one? What's wrong with me that the facilitator doesn't like me? To express particular affection in a group of people is not polite because you can hurt people that way.

Therefore, if you do experience affection for certain members of the group and would like to be close to them, then expressing what you feel becomes no insignificant challenge. You may very well hurt others. You may cause misunderstanding. You may be rejected. But you will have done what you are in the group to do : you will have been yourself to the extent that you could, and you will have given a model to others. Seeing that you are willing to hurt others in order to express what is really in you, others can find encouragement to try to be themselves even when side-effects are costly and against custom.

If you accept this freedom of being yourself even when it is affection you feel, you might, during the group, want to express that feeling in a way other than words. Although you will probably fear doing so, you might be moved to go to a person and put your hand on his shoulder, or take his hand in yours, or embrace him when he needs support. Often it is more difficult to express affection in this way, especially in a group. Walking across a room and touching the hand of another person or embracing him can require a good deal of courage and a mature freedom. But this, too, may be your way of helping the group simply by being yourself despite the cost.

It is easy to point out the risks, fears, and dangers involved if you break social rules and express individual affection for another individual in the group. But the good outcomes also deserve consideration. For example, in a one-day group, Alice, a woman in her mid-fifties, began to experience depression. She was a widow who was successfully working in a private social service organization. She was intelligent, efficient, and attractive. One of her co-workers, a man, was in the group. During the morning session he told Alice that at work she seemed aloof and domineering. He said that Alice very pleasantly wielded power over others in the organization. Her way of doing the work, while efficient, was the "only" way, and others working with her felt overlooked and pushed aside.

As she was hearing these accusations, Alice became angry. She felt misunderstood, and tried to explain her viewpoint. She told the young man that he had never tried to understand her, and that everyone in the organization seemed politely aloof. In her anger and self-defense, she threatened not to return to the group that day. When she did return late in the afternoon, no one said anything to her, although her hurt and depression were obvious.

At the final session in the evening, she arrived early and sat near another woman (a stranger to her before the group meetings) who, responding to Alice's depression, reached over and took her hand. Alice grasped and held the woman's hand for nearly half an hour as the group session proceeded. She said nothing. Finally the facilitator, noticing Alice's continuing anguish, asked her if she wished to say anything to the group. At this, Alice, in a strained voice, began to give reasons and theories about why she was upset. She explained about her good intentions at the place where she worked; she told of her loneliness, her devotion to others, her age and physical condition, her feeling of estrangement from her co-workers, her known success with persons who sought help from the organization. Explanation upon explanation for her depression tumbled from her fluent lips.

Suddenly the facilitator, moved with compassion and affection, walked across the room, leaned over, and embraced Alice. She rose, flung her arms around the man, and broke into sobs. The theories and reasons faded away before her human need for contact and love. Her coworker who had accused her earlier in the group came over and, with tears in his eyes, embraced her, and said he did care for her and he wished she would let "all of them at the office" be her friends.

Later the facilitator, whose embrace had broken through Alice's defenses, told her of the great fear he had experienced when he decided to walk across the room to her. He feared embracing a woman who might reject him, and he feared especially showing any affection to a particular person while he was facilitating a whole group. He feared hurting and alienating others. But, because the feeling was so strong "and embracing you seemed so hard, I pushed myself up and almost ran to you."

The aftermath of the group workshop was "raw and bloody" in Alice's own words, but she did begin both to give and to receive more affection and understanding. "I have my ups and downs, and sometimes things get quite strained; but somehow something is different. Things are better."

The Expression of Freedom

We have, in this chapter, considered that the most helpful way a facilitator can contribute to a group is to try to express his own feelings honestly, and to try to be himself despite the fears, risks, and demands that may accompany his attempts. If as facilitator you try to contribute in this way, you can expect that others in the group will take you as a model, and will begin themselves to risk exploring their own feelings and expressing them despite their fears.

Several persons may discover and examine feelings they did not know they had. One person may realize that he has much anger hidden in himself. Another may face fears he had only vaguely sensed before, but which had exercised strong control over his responses to others. Still another person, sure that he is the strong and brutal type, may begin to feel tenderness and affection, "soft" feelings he had kept hidden even from himself. Some may allow themselves for the first time in years to feel their own sorrow, their loneliness, or their compassion, or their shame, or their self-pity. Often these are emotions that they have considered bad or unworthy or socially unacceptable. Often these feelings are identified as part of the hidden inner self that must be kept from others for fear of causing disgust and rejection. Thanks to the example of the facilitator and others, a frightened person may gain courage to reveal this inner self. He sees that if he honestly explores his feelings he is not going to be destroyed or to destroy others. He sees that such honesty can, on the contrary, bring great relief to the person himself and can help others to feel more at home with him. Since such honesty is not commonly practiced in social circles, this person may not, before the group experience, have known what such honesty could bring about. He can look within himself and allow himself to experience a variety of emotions which he had previously closed off or left unexamined. This discovery and exploration of hidden emotions will sometimes shock the person, leave him bewildered, but at the same time bring him a sense of being reborn. The experience is usually not easy, but the facilitator's own "trying to be himself" is often a great help to the struggling person.

An example of discovery of feelings is the experience which a twenty-five-year-old woman underwent in an ongoing group that met for an hour a week over a period of three months. At the beginning of the group meetings, she appeared to others as charming and at ease. She was attractive and knew how to center attention on herself while at the same time encouraging others to speak of themselves. During subsequent sessions, to her own surprise, the woman began several times to mention fear. Finally, to the surprise of the whole group, a very perceptive man told the woman that he almost wished she would not come to the group anymore because the only emotion she seemed at home with was fear. The woman was shaken by this confrontation but, instead of contradicting the man, she said, "Maybe you are right. But I honestly didn't know I was so afraid. But I really am, I really am. I am very, very afraid."

Little by little, with the help of the group, she began to uncover her profound fear of people and of social failure. Although she had known something was bothering her, she had not been capable of identifying what it was. During later sessions of the group, she let herself painfully admit to her emotions of shame and unworthiness before others. She expressed, at real cost to herself, that she wanted affection but feared she could not inspire it. She allowed herself to recognize her fear of disapproval and condemnation from people she lived and worked with. She lived in fear of a constant and unfavorable "judgment" from known and unknown persons. By the end of the group meetings, she was far from being unafraid but she felt much more attuned to herself and began to have a new kind of trust in her own person. The discovery, exploration, and finally the acceptance of her fears was, in her own judgment, the major outcome of her group experience. She felt now she could "operate from a basis of realism."

The Fear of Freedom

Sometimes a person's difficulty is in expressing feelings he already knows he possesses. Out of fear or shame or because of social pressure, he disguises these feelings, and says to others what is basically insincere. Or he may say nothing when he wants very much to say what is in him. Sometimes he will code his feelings in the hope that the person will understand. The result of such silence or disguise is often that the person becomes dissatisfied with himself, and finds that he harbors in himself an explosive turbulence of unarticulated emotion. He may develop a façade of insincere responses, and keep his own self hidden.

If the facilitator is willing to express his own feelings despite his fears and despite the consequences of his expression, the person unable before to express himself may find opportunity and encouragement in the group situation to say things he has wanted for a long time to say. When the facilitator helps set such a tone of freedom and openness, then the group situation becomes a kind of special world in which persons can venture to be themselves, and can, as it were, practice an openness they desire to have in their daily lives. What are some of these feelings often left unexpressed? They are myriad, but among them are simple things, many of which a facilitator may find himself saying in the course of the group sessions. Perhaps a person has wished to say, "I like you," or "I'm glad we are friends," or "I do not like what you said," or "I am wondering why you want to talk so much," or "This conversation bores me," or "I hope we can become friends," or "Sorry, but I am a little depressed today," or, "I love you." The list is endless. These expressions are simple, but they remain for many persons insuperably difficult. A person wanting to say any one of them may have feared offending others and incurring their dislike. He may have feared revealing too much of himself, a self which shames him. He may have feared that the other person would meet his expression with silence, withdrawal, or rejection. He may have feared being thought weak, homosexual, or emotionally unstable. "People just don't say things like that." "You can't let a person know how you feel because he might take advantage of you."

But the facilitator can help by his own sincerity to create a special world where such expressions will be socially acceptable. Here, a person may take risks, try out the expressions, experience the varying responses from others, dissolve some of his own false notions, discover how much he can endure of honesty from others, feel what it is like to have someone address his real self and not his protective façade. The experience can be exhilarating and unforgettable. It can be dangerous and painful. It can bring joy and anguish. It can make a person close up more, or it can be the situation in which he discovers that the risks are worth it since it is so satisfying to be himself before others. How does the facilitator help? By trying himself to do what he hopes others will do—by trying to be honest in his expressions, by trying to become himself in the presence of others. If persons in the group have been able to interact honestly with one another and with the facilitator, then they will have had some practice for the far more difficult task of trying to be themselves in the daily world where they may not have many models of openness and sincerity. The facilitator will have done his job if he has created a climate in which each participant can discover and explore his own feelings, and can express these feelings to others as he has always wanted to do.

Example of a Group

It may be helpful to examine a group from the viewpoint of a counselor who joined a group in order to learn how to be a facilitator.

Steve, who had studied some counseling in graduate school, was a successful, ambitious young administrator doing remarkable work among students at a university. He seemed a man of character, casual in his approach both to students and to higher administrators. He seemed able to bridge differences, calm feelings, please almost everyone. Among his counseling problems was what he called the "one-shot interview" with parents of students who were to be suspended or who were failing in their work. As for his work with students themselves, he had begun to organize groups where students could air their differences and see where they stood in regard to, for example, certain policies of the administration. The groups seemed to be working, but Steve felt he needed more instruction in how to conduct successful groups. He decided to go across country to participate in a group led by a man Steve considered "the master." The group, consisting of twelve men and women from a variety of backgrounds, met for two sessions for five days. When Steve joined them the first morning, his sole intention consciously was to observe the technique of Charles, the master.

But at that first session, Charles said that he considered the group autonomous, free to do whatever the members wanted to do. "If you want to tell dirty jokes for the whole five days, that's all right with me." Then he told the participants what he had enjoyed most in the groups he had previously been facilitator for. "I have enjoyed it most when we have shared our feelings and helped one another grow." But he again said that these were his own feelings, and that he did not wish to impose them on this present group. "I do not wish to do anything to *lead* you in the normal sense of the word. I will just be myself in the group; at least that's all I want to be."

When Steve heard Charles's remarks, he discounted most of them. Charles, he thought, must have had some reason for saying such things; some underlying motive must be present. And so, not really believing the facilitator's words, Steve continued in his purpose of watching how "the master" ran the group. Steve was there, not for exploring his feelings, but for learning techniques. This attitude continued until the third day when a crisis arose. One of the women began to behave abnormally. She had, up to that time, attempted to elicit sympathy from the group and to exert control by such methods as reading long accounts of her feelings the day before. Most of the group members were irritated with her because they felt she was actually remaining aloof and hiding her real feelings in order to gain approval. On that third day one of the men expressed his irritation, and others joined in. After a heated exchange, the woman began sobbing and screaming. Finally, in rage she pushed away those trying to help her, threw herself on the floor and kicked. She repulsed every effort to be comforted or to talk out her exploding emotions. Soon everyone was both angry and frightened. The woman had complete control of the group. Everyone centered on her wild and frightening behavior.

Steve immediately looked to Charles. How would the master handle this display of abnormality? What techniques would he bring into play to calm the woman? Everyone was in panic; their plea to Charles was, "Do something!" But at the moment of panic, Steve saw Charles reflecting, looking inside to see what his feelings were. He was doing what he said was the most important thing he could do anytime. Then, after the moment's reflection, Charles shouted at the woman. He was really angry with her. He told her she was controlling the group by her wild behavior, and that he resented this. In his voice and demeanor there was no display of techniques for dealing with abnormal behavior. He was not the master psychologist employing his methods; he was, rather, what he had said he wanted to be—he was just Charles. Steve was profoundly affected by what he saw. From that moment on, he felt different in the group. He began to wonder what it would be like to "be Steve."

Earlier in the group, the only problems Steve had mentioned were his difficulties with the one-shot interview with parents of students who were in trouble. No one had a solution for him, but several said to him that he seemed closed up himself. "You can describe past feelings, but you don't seem in touch with yourself in the present moment." After the crisis situation, Steve did bring up a more personal problem. It concerned his reaction to the recent suicide of a student whom he had known fairly well. When Steve had been informed by phone of the suicide, he walked into his bedroom and locked the door. He had never before locked that door. This door-locking continued for several days after the suicide. He now asked the group to help him understand why he continued locking that door. "Was I locking the boy out?" No one had a solution. But finally a seventeen-year-old member of the group said, "Maybe, Steve, you were locking the boy *in,* not out. Maybe you wanted to tell him you really did care about him, and that you were sorry for the suicide."

This statement, for some reason or other, hit home. Steve suddenly began to experience anguish and sorrow. It was as if the emotions that he should have felt at the time of the suicide were now entering his consciousness. He was feeling them. But there seemed to be much more.

An overwhelming sadness came over him. At that moment he made the decision to look within himself and to let himself experience the feelings hidden within him. For nearly the whole two-hour session, he let himself feel and express his sorrows, terrors, regrets. He let himself experience immense self-pity. He felt that he was descending into a pit of frightful and unknown emotions which were only too obviously his own. "To be Steve" at that moment meant to hit rock-bottom in anguish, fear, and sorrow. The other group members helped him by their understanding and encouragement. Finally, for the first time in years, Steve began to cry. Little by little the weeping increased until he was sobbing. Then Charles rose from his seat, crossed the room and put his arm around Steve's shoulders. The gesture brought deep relief; Steve felt able to accept his feelings. The touch of Charles's arm communicated an affection and understanding that brought healing.

But, up to that moment, Charles had neither by word or gesture expressed affection for anyone in the group. When Steve was becoming more settled, two group members told Charles that they resented his gesture. "I felt hurt," one said, "because when I was feeling bad, you didn't embrace me. I feel you like Steve more than me, and I resent that. I feel you rejected me and other members of the group." Charles had no defense against this accusation. He said simply that he did what he wanted to do when he realized something of what Steve must be experiencing.

The experiences of that day changed the direction of Steve's life. Before a group of people he had revealed his weak and miserable self. Instead of rejecting him, almost everyone in the group, Charles especially, became closer than ever to him. It was all right for him to be himself. He was relieved of a large but previously unidentified burden. For the rest of the group sessions, he felt that he was in a semi-dream world. He knew that these people were his friends, and that he could trust them. He had never before experienced this kind of trust.

Afterwards, when he returned to his job, he felt that he had ceased living to please others and to make a name for himself. He had broken through to a new level of existence, one far more frightening and rich in emotion, but one more real and more rewarding. He later resigned his high-ranking administrative position to devote himself full-time to less lucrative individual and group counseling. He took a cut in both salary and prestige. But, more fundamentally, he began to take life as a challenge to be himself. He found that the day-to-day contact with others offered him constant risks. "Will I react in the old dishonest way, or will I, with this person, be myself? Will I be in touch with my real feelings, and attempt to hear and respond genuinely to this person with me right now? Will I risk letting him be himself?" Each day became an adventure. As for group work, Steve turned aside from manipulation and technique, and tried instead to indeed "follow the master" and be himself. Despite his eschewing ambition, he became a well-known, innovative, and successful group facilitator.

Conclusion

We have addressed this book to those humanly attractive people whom persons in need seek out for understanding. These counselors may have little or no professional training in psychology; but they have the human feelings and responses that attract the troubled person. Their counseling qualification is their own humanity. To the person needing help, the natural counselor, who might be a nurse or a teacher or a lawyer or a friend, is "someone to tell my troubles to." Some human quality in the counselor promises understanding and assistance.

When the person in need approaches the counselor, his expectations may be vague and uncertain. He may not consciously know what he wants. It is our belief that underneath his surface problems lies a search for a human relationship. The client wants not merely to "tell his troubles," but to tell his troubles to an understanding, receptive, and responsive human being. The client wants to enter a relationship with another person. In the person he selects as his counselor he has sensed the presence of those qualities that would encourage such a relationship. In our view, developing such a relationship between counselor and client is central to the success of the counseling. What is required is that the counselor be for this person, not a professional help-giver, but himself—this complex, imperfect, somewhat unpredictable but sincere human being whose humanness attracted the client.

Yet it is all too easy for the counselor to downplay these very human qualities when a person in need confronts him. He may retreat into his fears about counseling. "I don't know what I'm supposed to say." Thanks to these fears, he may so distrust his human qualities that he hides them and assumes the role of what he thinks a counselor ought to be. For him the client ceases to be a person asking for a human response, and becomes instead a problem to be studied and solved. Suddenly it becomes most important to decide whether the student should change his major, or the patient should be released from the hospital early, or the legal client should make out his will at another time. In assuming his helper role, the counselor overlooks his real counseling qualifications— the human feelings and responses which drew the client to him in the first place. By distrusting his own humanity, the counselor blocks the development of the human relationship that is the fundamental need of the client.

It is our view that counseling will have a far better chance of success when the counselor allows himself to share with the client those qualities that make him, not a problem-solver, but a human being. We believe that his being human before someone in emotional turmoil will best help that person find the peace he is searching for. But it is not easy to be transparent about the qualities that make us human. Many of these qualities seem to be embarrassing or shameful weaknesses. Like everyone else, the counselor finds it hard to express many of his real feelings and responses. For anyone, self-revelation, even of affection and concern, is a frightening venture. If the average person can think of many reasons why he should not communicate honestly with others, the counselor seems to have even more reasons to remain silent about his emotional reactions to the person seeking help. A counselor can fear that if he expresses his annoyance at his client's compulsive talking, or his fear of his client's suicide threats, or his discomfort with his client's homosexual tendencies, he will increase the turmoil that is already so severe.

It is our hope that the human counselor will express himself honestly in spite of his fears. We feel that in this way the client will have the opportunity to discover that his own emotional upset is rooted, not in some terrible abnormality, but in his being human. Thanks to the counselor's honesty about himself, the client can see that his own turmoil is in reality everyone's turmoil. The client can discover that the only difference between him and others is that he has allowed himself to be overwhelmed with the feelings and reactions that others seem to handle with relative ease. The client finds that he is not alone in having these feelings. Such a realization can bring great relief and encouragement. This help comes, not from professionalism, but from another human being who openly shared his own human reactions with the client.

The counselor who shares his humanity with his client begins to establish a bond of friendship. The bond grows as the two persons share their common emotional reactions. It is the counselor who is willing to risk self-revelation who can expose the client to this experience of friendship. The experience heals; but it also exposes the client to the fears, the risks, and the rewards of friendship. The counselor will probably suffer the difficulties of involvement with this person. The client may experience dependency with all its powers and threats. If the two persons continue to be honest with themselves and with each other, they will be able to cope with these perils of friendship even as they deepen its bond. Through this experience fraught with difficulty, the client discovers what it means to give and receive friendship. He discovers many ways in which he has previously failed in his relationships. Above all, he receives new confidence in the worth of his own person and in his ability to relate satisfactorily to others. Another person has accepted and responded to him with esteem and affection. The human counselor, then, is not content with explaining how to relate to others; he demonstrates the experience by entering into it with the person seeking help.

Sometimes the natural counselor will be asked to be a leader or facilitator or counselor of a group of persons. In the group situation often both the counselor and the other members will find the ultimate test of their ability to know and express themselves honestly. If it is hard to speak to just one other person of the emotions we all tend to hide, then the ultimate challenge is to reveal this hidden self before a whole group. We are pressed to be the same person before everyone. But if the counselor can do this, he has, in our opinion, made his most valuable contribution to the group. His bravery and sincerity will encourage others to take the risks of truthful expression. Such sharing of the self can make the group a successful experience. For in our view the ultimate goal of group counseling, as of all counseling, is to help another person discover, accept, and live the person he truly is.

This book is incomplete until we mention our debt of gratitude to the many people who have sought our help over the years. It is their courage, honesty, and sincerity that inspires these pages. We are also grateful to the many counselors from all walks of life who generously shared their personal experiences with us. Among these counselors, we owe a special note of thanks to Professor Thomas L. Shaffer, dean of the University of Notre Dame Law School, for his advice and encouragement.